Shakespeare's Sonnets

Self, Love and Art

Shakespeare's Sonnets

Self, Love and Art

PHILIP MARTIN

Senior Lecturer in English
Monash University, Melbourne

CAMBRIDGE

At the University Press

1972

Published by the Syndics of the Cambridge University Press
Bentley House, 200 Euston Road, London NW1 2DB
American Branch: 32 East 57th Street, New York, N.Y.10022

© Cambridge University Press 1972

Library of Congress Catalogue Card Number: 73–189593

ISBN 0 521 08525 X

Printed in Great Britain
by W & J Mackay Limited, Chatham

TO MY MOTHER
AND TO THE MEMORY OF MY GRANDFATHER
FRANK TALBOT

Contents

Preface

I should like to thank those who have helped in the writing of this book. What it owes to the published works of critics and scholars can be gauged from references made to them in the text, and from the bibliography. Equally my thanks are due to a number of other people, mostly colleagues and friends in Australia.

Among those who were with me at the University of Melbourne: to Joanne Lee Dow, A.D. Moody, T.B. Tomlinson, Robin Grove and, in particular, Jennifer Gribble, who not only made helpful comments on a late draft but prompted me to study the Sonnets in the first place. At the Australian National University, Canberra: to A.D. Hope and F.H. Langman. In England: to Winifred Nowottny, of University College, London. At Monash University: to colleagues and students for much worthwhile discussion, to Maureen Mann who checked aspects of the final manuscript, and to Elizabeth Moore who typed it, with assistance from Heather Phillips.

Two sections of this work have appeared in print before, both in *The Critical Survey*: the study of Shakespeare's Sonnet 94 (Summer 1969) and the study of Donne's 'Twicknam Garden' (Summer 1970). I should like to thank the editors for allowing me to include these sections in this book.

March 1972   PHILIP MARTIN

Introduction

In a recent book, Stephen Booth has expressed quite simply what many readers have found: 'Shakespeare's sonnets are hard to think about. They are hard to think about individually and they are hard to think about collectively.'[1] For this reason it is no use projecting a grand scheme in an essay as short as this. I shall not attempt to give a comprehensive picture of the whole sequence: many sonnets will not be mentioned at all, while others will be discussed at considerable length and in some cases more than once. I have had to abandon early hopes of making extended comparisons between the Sonnets and Shakespeare's other works: references to these are occasional only, and brief. It seems best to consider the Sonnets in their immediate context, in the context, that is, of the short Elizabethan love poem, particularly the love sonnet and more especially the work of Sidney, Daniel, Drayton and Spenser, the other chief poets who used the form. Shakespeare's Sonnets, after all, make up one of the sonnet-sequences of the 1590s, even if they were not published until nearly a decade after the craze had died down, and even if in many ways they are strikingly different from the rest.

I assume that Shakespeare wrote his sonnets, or most of them, during the nineties, though we cannot be certain

---

[1] Stephen Booth, *An Essay on Shakespeare's Sonnets* (New Haven and London, 1969), p. 1.

I

about this. For the most part they read like fairly early work; some of them were undoubtedly in circulation by 1599, since versions of Sonnets 138 and 144 appeared in *The Passionate Pilgrim* in that year; and it seems likely that it was to the Sonnets we have, or to some of them, that Francis Meres referred in 1598, in his famous phrase about Shakespeare's 'sugred Sonnets among his private friends'.[1] The word 'private' suggests not only that the poems were circulating in manuscript according to the common practice but that Shakespeare may have wished them to be kept like that: they were, perhaps, like so many of the Sonnets we know as his, intimate in tone and reference, intended for a few eyes only. Further, it seems likely that the *Shake-speares Sonnets* of 1609 appeared without Shakespeare's authority,[2] which does something to indicate that those poems may well be the ones which Meres had seen or heard of.

But all this, in Sir Thomas Browne's words, is a matter of 'but wavering conjecture'. The dating of the Sonnets, like so much else about them, has not been settled and probably never will be. Their date is of some importance, of course, especially if one wants to establish their relation to other works by Shakespeare, such as *Love's Labour's Lost*, *Measure for Measure* or *Troilus and Cressida*, or to works by other poets, such as certain sonnets by Sidney, Daniel and Spenser which Shakespeare may have imitated or, in Spenser's case, inspired. Or to take the famous line in Sonnet 94 about 'lilies that fester': did Shakespeare write the sonnet before or after the line was used in *Edward III*, and if Shakespeare himself wrote the scene in which it occurs, was he quoting the sonnet or does the sonnet quote the play? One would of

---

[1] Francis Meres, *Palladis Tamia* (1598), quoted in *Shakespeare's Sonnets*, ed. Martin Seymour-Smith (London, 1963), p. 4.

[2] *A New Variorum Edition of Shakespeare: The Sonnets*, ed. H. E. Rollins (Philadelphia and London, 1944), vol. II, pp. 1–18.

course be glad to know for certain when the Sonnets were written: it could enable us to read them better. But as it is, we must proceed on what seems a reasonable if approximate calculation: I should say, *c.* 1593 to *c.* 1603 at the outside, and perhaps not so late.

In any case, it is not of crucial importance. The same may be said more strongly of other questions on which so much has been written, and which I mention only to dismiss as irrelevant to this study: Who was the Young Man? Who was the Rival Poet? Who was the Dark Lady? The weariness of spirit shown by Rollins in his Variorum edition of the Sonnets testifies to the vanity and vexation of so many generations and volumes of debate; and the material he has assembled, the infinite variety of the hypotheses put forward by commentator after commentator, sounds its own grave warning. The identities of the three people are not known, very probably they can never be known, and for a reading of the Sonnets as poetry they are of little or no importance. I shall not discuss whether the Fair Friend is Southampton, or Pembroke, or any of the other young pretenders; nor whether the Rival Poet is Marlowe, or Chapman, or another; much less grope about for the name of the Dark Lady, which, of the three, is the one we are least likely ever to know. Obviously, critical judgments must rest on sound scholarship, but the scholarship available on this subject, even more than on the dating of the Sonnets, leaves us in much doubt. Of the three people nothing is known, but nothing need be known, beyond the characters and characteristics attributed to them by the Sonnets themselves. Their names may not be there, but what they *are*, what they mean to the poet and sometimes to one another, what they must mean to us, is written into the poems. The friend, for example, may or may not have been Southampton, but in and for the poems there is no doubt what sort of person he is: young, beautiful, narcissistic and in some sense an aristocrat, someone with the attitudes, likeable or not, of those that have power. No one can know exactly what situation it was that Shakespeare's imagination worked on to produce the relationship between the poet and the friend. William Empson has offered an ingenious account[1] of how that imagination conceivably worked. Assuming that the relations given by the Sonnets are the same as the biographical ones – young aristocrat and ageing admirer of lower rank – he shows how in *Henry IV* the friend is transformed into Prince Hal and the poet into Falstaff. It is quite plausible, and anyone who has written the most modestly successful poem or story knows how curiously his material may come together: something from his present combining with something from his past, something experienced in daily life with something felt in the reading of a book, or an actual situation becoming inverted or reversed, so that the roles of two people in life may be subtly exchanged in the work of art. It is possible that the situation in Shakespeare's life was that of the Sonnets, as Empson assumes (and with him so many less acute commentators). It is also possible, as my colleague F. H. Langman has suggested to me, that in the Sonnets Shakespeare has reversed the roles: finding himself perhaps loved by a man older than himself, he puts himself in that man's position. The flexible imagination which created the plays is quite capable of this. The point of the suggestion, however, was not to form yet another theory about the story behind the Sonnets, but to stress the futility of the whole approach and to draw attention away from the raw material, which we cannot know and which

---

[1] William Empson, 'They that have power' in *Some Versions of Pastoral* (Harmondsworth, 1966), pp. 75–96.

cannot help us, towards the poems themselves. If only more of the commentators were as sensible as the mid-nineteenth-century editor, Robert Bell: 'All poetry is auto-biographical. But the particle of actual life out of which verse is wrought may be, and almost always is, wholly incommensurate to the emotion depicted, and remote from the forms into which it is ultimately shaped.'[1] And as M.M. Mahood adds: 'Some trifle light as air may have rendered Shakespeare the man jealous of a friend's affection and so created the tormented "I" of the sonnets as well as the two Antonios and certain aspects of Falstaff.'[2] It is with the creations alone that I am concerned.

Two other questions often raised are not so easily dismissed, and neither can be given a simple answer. One is whether the Quarto of 1609 gives the Sonnets in their right order, and the other is whether the Sonnets form a sequence or merely a collection. In some respects the questions are related. As for the first, it is clear that in certain instances the order has almost certainly been upset in the Quarto, if 'order' is taken to mean a narrative or emotional progression. The most striking instances occur among the sonnets to the mistress. It is odd to find 130, 'My Mistres eyes are nothing like the Sunne', immediately following 'Th'expence of Spirit in a waste of shame', and one can only say that whatever the order in which the poems were written, this does not strike us as the order of feeling, the order of their 'psychological necessity'.[3] It is not that the two poems form a contrast: that, of course, might well be part of an artistic effect. Instead they are simply at odds, thrown into uneasy

---

[1] Quoted by Rollins, vol. II, p. 139.
[2] M.M. Mahood, 'Love's Confin'd Doom' in *Shakespeare Survey* 15 (1962), p. 61.
[3] Tucker Brooke's phrase, quoted by Edward Hubler in *The Sense of Shakespeare's Sonnets* (New York, 1952), p. 38.

company. 'Th'expence of Spirit' is out of place and premature here: the relationship revealed by the poems on either side of it is not yet profound enough to yield such an intense and troubled poem. Nevertheless, I shall not attempt, as many have done, to rearrange the Sonnets. I accept the order of the Quarto *faute de mieux*, while noting that some poems seem in that edition to be misplaced. I am more concerned with themes and poetic quality than with the progression of a story or even with the emotional or psychological development traced by the Sonnets. It strikes me, however, that the order of the first 126 sonnets, to the friend, is more plausible than that of the group to the mistress. The first group (or two groups: 1–17, 18–126) could well be in the order of composition which is at the same time the order of feeling, with all the likely fluctuations and veerings of the imagination. But in any case, since we don't *know* what Shakespeare's order was, we may as well accept the order of the Quarto.[1]

As for the second question – sequence or collection? – again no satisfactory answer can be given. The Sonnets are more than a collection, certainly, but what kind of a sequence do they form? One which is not very tidy or carefully planned, and at some points more sequential than at others. No one could miss, for instance, the close-knit unity of the first seventeen, or the continuous movement formed by 71–4. There are sequences within the larger sequence: the sonnets to the friend, the sonnets to the mistress; but these are not completely self-contained. They do illuminate

---

[1] The text I have used throughout this study is that of Martin Seymour-Smith (London, 1963), which, except for occasional amendments recorded in footnotes, follows the Quarto in order, spelling and punctuation. Wherever 'Seymour-Smith' is mentioned I am referring to this volume, and in most cases to the introduction and the commentary which accompany the text.

6

each other, though to what extent this was Shakespeare's conscious intention it is hard to know. There are, too, as I have just suggested, minor sequences within these two major ones: poems exploring a phase of the relationship or developing a line of reflection which it has prompted (for example the three sonnets on the friend's fault, 33-5, or the self-analytical sonnets, 109-11). To what extent should each poem be read on its own, to what extent is it intended to give meaning to its group and take meaning from it, to what extent does one group throw light on another, or the whole body of the Sonnets on an individual poem? While it is not possible to give cut-and-dried answers and one must take each case separately, as a general rule I shall try to judge each sonnet as an entity, even if it forms part of a group, and shall resist calling in one sonnet to support another which seems unable to stand up alone.

It must be added that if the Sonnets form a sequence we still face the difficulty of taking in all of them at once. I suspect that not many readers try, and that of those who do, some abandon the attempt. If so, it does not necessarily reflect on them or on the poems, for as C.L. Barber says:

To read through the sonnets at a sitting, though it is useful for surveying the topography they present, does violence to them and to the reader–it can produce a sensation of hothouse oppression. Each poem needs to be dwelt on; each requires the kind of concentrated attention which could have been given when they were received singly or in small groups. To read and reread is essential if we are to enjoy the way each moves, the use it makes of the possibilities of the sonnet form, the particular development in it of a design of sounds and images. The sonnets ask for a special sort of attention because in them poetry is, in a special way, an action.[1]

This, like other comments of Barber's, seems to me apt and

[1] C.L. Barber, 'An Essay on the Sonnets' in *The Sonnets* (Laurel Shakespeare), (New York, 1962), p. 11.

perceptive; certainly it represents my own experience of the poems. In what follows I shall, as Barber suggests, dwell on some of them, not only to see how each moves, how each uses the form, but more generally to discover the kind of poetic life which each gives to its subject. This will involve a good deal of close attention to the language and especially to its 'wordplay', the fruitfulness of its quibbling, since, as John Dover Wilson reminds us (*contra* Dr Johnson):

Shakespeare habitually thought in quibbles, if indeed 'quibble' be the right term for what was one of the main roots of his poetic expression. When he used a word, all possible meanings of it were commonly present to his mind, so that it was like a musical chord which might be resolved in whatever fashion or direction he pleased. To miss a quibble, then, is often to miss the interwoven thread which connects together a whole train of images; for imagery and double meaning are generally inseparable.[1]

Since the Sonnets are so numerous and so dense, one must decide which aspects of the sequence and which specific poems to concentrate on. The main concerns of the sequence can readily be listed: love, time, death, all that is meant by 'mutability', and the means available to transcend it – begetting children and creating poetry. It is more difficult to trace adequately the links between these main themes in the poetry itself. The concern with love, for instance, takes in self-love as well, and that in turn has more than one aspect. 'Self-love' can mean two things and not, as we commonly think, one only: self-love may be a destructive habit, time-wasting and self-wasting, an 'all-eating shame' in the words of Sonnet 2, but as Erich Fromm insists in his book *The Art of Loving*,[2] it may also be a necessary virtue. The Sonnets deal with both of these, not only with the first. Time, too, can be seen doubly: as 'eater of youth'

[1] J. Dover Wilson (ed.), *Hamlet* (Cambridge, 1936), Introduction, p. xxxv.
[2] Erich Fromm, *The Art of Loving* (London, 1966), pp. 45–9.

but also as the condition in which man can get 'increase' by wedding Beauty to Use. He can choose either to defy death or to die twice by not living creatively, that is, by not building his monument in his children. In this context the role of the poet is to erect other monuments, but neither in stone nor in flesh: poems, which will commemorate the self who made them and still more the other self whom he loved.

Shakespeare's feeling for selfhood, it seems to me, underlies the whole body of the Sonnets; it is implied in his concern with poetry, with mutability, above all with love, and it is uncommon in the love poetry of the time. It is often said that in the Sonnets he is much concerned with narcissism, and so he is, but this is only part of the larger concern to which I am pointing. The Sonnets reveal and create many intricate and shifting patterns among their many preoccupations. My main purpose in this study is to explore one pattern in which self, love and art are related to each other.

I begin with two chapters on sonnets which deal with what Sonnet 62 calls 'sin of self-love'. The first chapter deals with sonnets on the youth, the second with sonnets on the poet himself. I want to show both what these poems are like individually and how they embody characteristic preoccupations that recur throughout the sequence. The poet's own self-examination, considered in chapter 2, implies not self-hatred but a feeling for the value of the self, a value which certain experiences can erode. Hence the particular relevance, to the general theme, of the Dark Lady sequence, where, counterbalancing the youth's narcissism which is the theme of the first group (1–17) and of many poems in the second (18–126), the poet faces his own partial destruction of himself.

9

This leads in the third chapter to a discussion of Shakespeare's sense of a positive self-love. I think he would have agreed with Fromm that the Biblical injunction to 'Love thy neighbour as thyself' makes little sense if one does not love oneself as well: in Sir Thomas Browne's words, once more, 'How shall we expect Charity towards others, when we are uncharitable to ourselves?' In the early sonnets the self-regarding youth is said to be 'possest with murdrous hate', and Shakespeare later applies the same insight to himself. In positive terms, Shakespeare's sense of selfhood can be seen in the awareness he always conveys of his own being, even in sonnets where he seems to abase himself completely, to confess that he is 'passion's slave': here, very often, what looks at first like total loss of self-respect turns out to be something very different. A frequently ironic awareness of his predicament subtly but genuinely reverses that predicament, enables him to transcend it. We can see this in a poem like Sonnet 57:

> Being your slave what should I doe but tend,
> Upon the houres, and times of your desire?
> I have no precious time at al to spend;
> Nor services to doe til you require,

where the characteristically sly balancing of tones, the unobtrusive but calculated exaggerations, suggest a detached awareness, and assessment, of the very weakness the poem confesses.

It is this multiple awareness, both of different possibilities in himself and of the selfhood of others, this patient but not (finally) passive acceptance of the truth, which characterize the love that Shakespeare professes; a love that recognizes selfhood even while it is prepared to give the self unreservedly to another: 'for I love you so,/That I in your sweet thoughts would be forgot'. Paradoxically this self-forgetfulness still indicates a form of self-love: the poet is able to flow out of himself and therefore to be more fully himself: 'To give away your selfe, keeps your selfe still', as he tells the youth. And it is this kind of *love* on the part of the poet-figure of the Sonnets which makes possible the kind of *poetry* Shakespeare writes, here and ultimately in all his work: a point taken up in chapter 5.

The second half of chapter 3 examines some of the great love sonnets, in order to show how various this love and these sonnets are. In the following, portmanteau chapter I consider first of all why Renaissance poets, and Shakespeare in particular, should have used the sonnet form so often, and also why and in what ways a large number of Shakespeare's own sonnets are imperfect. Secondly I consider the work of the four chief sonneteers other than Shakespeare, examining both their poetic achievement and the view of love which they offer. This means looking at their use of the Petrarchan convention and at the original dignity and stature of Petrarch's own conception of the mistress, something of which is to be glimpsed in an unfinished poem of Ralegh's, discussed briefly at the outset of the survey.

This sketch of Elizabethan love poetry should serve as a context for the comparison of Shakespeare and Donne which follows in chapter 5. As Patrick Cruttwell argues in his stimulating book *The Shakespearean Moment*, these are the two great poets of their time, and their pre-eminence is seen in their love poetry as well as elsewhere. In this chapter I discuss what they have to say about conventional poetic love and about the psychological and emotional realities which, by contrast, they find in actual experience. I want to show that both poets were thoroughly aware of the love conventions, used them as far as they were useful but no further, and were often critical of them: sometimes by implication and almost, it seems, by accident, sometimes quite overtly, as in 'My Mistres eyes are nothing like the Sunne' and in 'Twicknam Garden'. Such poems direct their attack at something falsifying, even demeaning, in much conventional love poetry. In Shakespeare's poem the target is little more than a way of writing; in Donne's, which is more probing, it is the way of feeling which that way of writing portrays. So many mistresses, Shakespeare says, are 'beli'd with false compare': *his* mistress's looks are unfashionable, but she is real. Donne's Petrarchan lover, in his unmanly wretchedness, wishes himself something less than human, a mandrake or a stone fountain, because he cannot bear to leave off loving. Both poets, with their sense of the ridiculous, assert the standard of common sense, of human reality; both have a sense of the human person in love. What they show of the nature of love can be traced to their sense of the self; the sense of it which underlies most contemporary love poetry is false, shallow and even trivial.

This fifth chapter ends by comparing the two poetic sensibilities, poetic selves, of Shakespeare and Donne: alike in many of their insights, as in their shared pre-eminence as the greatest love poets of their age, they are nonetheless different in some of their chief qualities. Two kinds of self emerge: Donne's the more assertive, the more obviously 'dramatic', Shakespeare's the more modest, more self-effacing, one might say the more humble. It is often enough pointed out that although Donne's poems are compressed dramas, he would probably not have made a good playwright. The reason for this seems to be that however diverse the moods and attitudes of the poems, their central figure is nearly always Donne himself. Shakespeare, by contrast, is much less self-insistent. The Sonnets *do* what the poet *says* about forgetting himself. And while they don't actually show, in its full force, what Keats, with Shakespeare in mind, called 'the poetical character' ('it is not itself – it has no self...A Poet...is continually...filling some other Body', etc.),[1] they do show the nature of the genius which was to produce the great plays. The Sonnets' very openness and modesty, the self-abnegation they speak of, are the condition of Shakespeare's achievement as a dramatist. The lover in the Sonnets is, in effect, a figure of the poet as Keats describes him, and in a manner that we never find in Donne. We may be surprised at first that there is so little self-dramatization in the Sonnets, but this is to be expected in the love lyrics of a man with an extraordinary gift for empathy, for 'continually filling some other Body'. It is the plays which show how fully he possessed that gift; but the poems, too, bear witness to it, in their own way.

In the final chapter, certain implications of this and of earlier chapters are taken up and extended. Love, as the poet finds it, has some power to resist the universal flux; it is 'builded far from accident', it can 'bear it out even to the edge of doom'. But, to use Fromm's terminology, love by its nature is productive: and if the youth must get a child, what is the poet's proper mode of love? Clearly enough, poetry. What sort of poetry, then, does the poet of the Sonnets -- and, with him, Shakespeare – make? Clearly, again, poetry which seeks to immortalize the beloved. But how can poetry do that? And precisely what did Shakespeare, along with other poets of his time, believe he was doing when he claimed that his verse would confer immortality? Not, surely, that he was giving a *portrait* of the beloved, for few sonnets, if any, even attempt one. The Sonnets talk a good deal about the power of poetry to

---

[1] Letter to Richard Woodhouse, 27 October 1818, in *Letters of John Keats*, ed. H. E. Rollins (Cambridge, Mass., 1958), vol. I, pp. 386–7.

triumph over time and death; and sometimes it seems *mere* talk. The nature of the attempt, and its success in various sonnets, need to be examined. The chapter (and the study) ends with Sonnet 55 ('Not marble, nor the guilded monuments'), which more than any other sonnet actually does what it says. It is a 'builded' and a 'powreful rime'. And besides *being* a monument in verse (and not just talking about being one), it recognizes, as no other poem of its kind does, the independent existence of the beloved and of other lovers throughout the remainder of history:

> So til the judgement that your selfe arise,
> You live in this, and dwell in lovers eies.

I

Sin of Self-Love: the Youth

Anyone who reads the Sonnets must notice how often and how variously they speak of self-love. It is there from the start. The order of the Quarto may be disputed, but surely not the position of Sonnet 1. For the sequence could have no opening so completely Shakespearean as this. Here, as in those dialogues between minor characters which open many of the great plays, the chief themes are quietly asserted: the youth's beauty, the destructiveness of time, the choice to be made between defying time and co-operating with it.

> From fairest creatures we desire increase,
> That thereby beauties *Rose* might never die,
> But as the riper should by time decease,
> His tender heire might beare his memory:
> But thou contracted to thine owne bright eyes,
> Feed'st thy lights flame with selfe substantiall fewell,
> Making a famine where aboundance lies,
> Thy selfe thy foe, to thy sweet selfe too cruell:
> Thou that art now the worlds fresh ornament,
> And only herauld to the gaudy spring,
> Within thine owne bud buriest thy content,
> And tender chorle makst wast in niggarding:
>   Pitty the world, or else this glutton be,
>   To eate the worlds due, by the grave and thee.

What particularly corresponds here to the first scenes of the plays is the pitch of the poetry, the understatement of its manner. This is a deliberately minor sonnet as compared, say, with 'Not marble, nor the guilded monuments' or 'Let me not to the marriage of true mindes'. It is not elevated, it is not one of the great moments of the sequence, yet it is indispensable. And while it is, like Sonnet 144 ('Two loves I have of comfort and dispaire'), an obviously thematic sonnet, it does not merely state its themes, it embodies them in a respectably complex poetic texture. Restrained as it is, it has the true Shakespearean richness of suggestion. And to read it aloud will show how beautifully timed its long crescendo is; how much the aural shape of the poem, its 'music' in the popular sense, is a part of that other 'music of poetry' which Eliot speaks of: the patterning of diverse, even discordant elements into a unified meaning.

Self-love may be servitude, self-love may be freedom: this is what a great many of the Sonnets say, some throwing the emphasis on one possibility, some on the other. In Sonnet 1 it falls on the first: self-love, as the poet sees it in the youth, is nothing less than a complicity with 'devouring Time'. But the point is made both tellingly and winningly; praise and condemnation balance each other. This is a poetry which keeps something in reserve and never raises its voice unless it has to. The 'thou' of the poem is not mentioned a moment too soon, and the harshest word applied to him, 'glutton', is held back until the second last line, where the rhythm gives it a surprising force. But it would be well to look more closely at this sonnet to see what it establishes, not only in the way of themes, but also of modes of language; for in both respects (which are in any case intimately related) it is a genuine introduction to the poems that follow.[1]

---

[1] I am indebted at various points to Winifred Nowottny's valuable study of 'Formal Elements in Shakespeare's Sonnets: Sonnets I–VI' in Barbara Herrnstein (ed.), *Discussions of Shakespeare's Sonnets* (Boston, 1964), pp. 152–8.

The first line intimates a concern with 'creatures', beings subject to a mightier power (though that is not yet insisted on); and by assonance and alliteration 'creatures' and 'increase' are linked in the poetry as they should be (the poem implies) in life. 'Thereby' in line 2 points back, more than syntactically, to 'increase' and to the 'creatures' from which it proceeds. As an image, 'beauties *Rose*' needs no more force than it has, being used as a commonplace for beauty perpetually flourishing, withering and being re-born. The line goes on to introduce the ideas of *dying* and of *never dying*, and thus to make the first reference to immortality. In line 3 the suggestions of 'as...should' are ambiguous. The line points to what *must* happen in the nature of things, with which it seems prepared to acquiesce: that 'the riper should by time decease' is fitting. But (the next line adds) only if there is an heir. And this changes the meaning of 'as' from 'because' to 'while' in both its senses: firstly as referring to time (while one life is declining, an-other rises in its stead) and secondly as marking a contrast (on the one hand, death; on the other, new life patterned on the old). And together the two lines juxtapose 'riper' and 'tender'. 'Riper' has the usual Shakespearean associations of maturity and acceptance ('Ripeness is all'), and there may be an implication, coming partly from the even move-ment of the line, that the acceptance is that of the parent as well as of people generally (the 'we' of the poem): for him it is a 'well-contented day', or it will be if an heir survives it. And a 'tender' heir: the word implying youth (the first blades of grass, the first shoots on a bough), and also human affection, the grateful love of children towards those who have given them life, and whose memory they are glad to 'beare'. The delicate forwarding movement of the language is difficult to suggest in critical prose: it is so much more deftly many-sided than any description can be. As Mrs Nowottny remarks, in discussing the fugal form of Sonnet 4, 'critical analysis, which cannot reproduce the simultaneousness of the original, must labour heavily behind, discussing first the development of each part and then their interaction' (p. 155). But even such an attempt may suggest how one line leads inevitably into the next, and in no mechanical or predictable way; how even the second half of a line may realize a further stage of the process established in the first. The furthering may be achieved, as we have seen, by an ambiguous phrase or by a pun on a single word: 'beare', for instance. Essentially the line in which this occurs is concerned with issue: an heir who will carry on the parent's line. But the poetry does not separate biology from the rest of life. 'Beare his memory' conveys the two ideas that in his love the heir consciously cherishes the memory of his father, that in himself he *is* the memory of his father, whose image can be seen in him by those (like the poet perhaps?) who knew the father; and that naturally the son will wish to carry on his memory, his *and* his father's, by begetting children of his own.

The first quatrain, then, creates a sense of natural and inevitable order, a necessary enchainment of one generation with the next and the next: father, child, and the unconceived who must be brought to birth. This quatrain states the thesis both of this sonnet and of at least the sixteen poems which follow it. I would point again to the quietness of this opening: a softly-spoken but in no way tentative statement of an idea which (the tone leads us to feel) no one is likely to deny. There is tact here (or is it tactics?); and there is, too, an expansive movement within the quatrain. The first line provides a starting-point as quiet and gentle as possible, but each line seems to mount on the rising curve of the one before it, and the gradually mounting wave of the four lines together sweeps us slowly but powerfully into the second quatrain. If the first states a thesis the second shows its immediate application. We know we have reached the point of reference with the first words: 'But *thou*'. And yet in the next words the gentleness of the poem's manner, or manners, is still apparent. No ringing denunciation, at least not yet. Instead:

> But thou contracted to thine owne *bright eyes*,
> Feed'st thy *lights flame* with *selfe substantiall fewell*,
> Making a famine where aboundance lies.

Half of the effect of these lines is of praise for the youth. Beyond doubt the compliment is intended: his eyes *are* bright. If it is becoming clear that he falls short of his end, the lines intimate also the wealth of his endowments. It is *almost* pardonable, certainly understandable, that he should live as he does, with such eyes, such abundance, to 'court an amorous looking-glass'; the poetry, pursuing this vein of compliment, might almost seem to be saying that the youth is, as he thinks, 'selfe substantiall'. Yet in this process the self is being consumed. And the vein that runs counter to that of praise emerges strongly in the third line with the heavy stress on 'famine'; so that the negative is already set against the positive at the climax of the quatrain and the centre of the poem. Quite effortlessly the poetry holds in one hand the two terms of the contradiction: in 'Making a famine where aboundance lies', the rhythmic antithesis between 'famine' and 'aboundance' weighs praise against blame, blame against praise, and in a manner to suggest that an abundance which 'lies' unused must turn to a famine equally great; a destruction equal to the power destroyed. The quatrain ends with a paradox which, through a lessened subtlety, creates I think a slight anticlimax even while it drives the point home; yet the two strands are retained, of criticism and compliment, or rather, perhaps, of appeal: 'Thy selfe thy foe, to thy *sweet* selfe too *cruell*'.

This double insistence is carried through into the third quatrain. The beloved is 'now the worlds fresh ornament': 'fresh' on the one hand meaning new, young, vital, and on the other implying, with some help from 'now', that possibly the world has had other such ornaments before, and will lose this just as it lost those: You won't always be beautiful. And (say the next two lines) if I call you 'herauld to the gaudy spring' I mean that while you seem to promise new life and growth, in fact you frustrate it: 'within thine owne bud buriest thy content'. Not that the verse makes any crude opposition: the youth *is* the world's fresh ornament *and* he buries his own content. 'Content' means 'all that he contains', which of course includes the power to beget children, and at the same time it means his 'contentment', now and more especially in the future, and the contentment which he could give to others. 'Bury' has something of the sense it has in 'burying one's talents' or 'burying one's head in the sand' as well as conveying the more important, more direct meaning that the youth is making an end, and so a grave, of that which is properly the beginning of new life, his 'owne bud'. We are offered a paradox which underlies most of the sonnets, and all of the sonnets on this theme: that to concentrate on your self is to lose it. For it can't be kept: if it is not given away it will be taken away. The friend may be a bud, but he can flower only in another. To swerve from this is to make waste in niggarding: to squander one's substance through sheer meanness, or to be guilty of a kind of gluttony. Now in the couplet we are made to see new meaning in the word 'feed' of line 6. There it referred to the fuelling of a fire. Here the reference is human: gluttony means eating more than one needs, and perhaps what others need; so to consume oneself is to consume what, in one's issue, belongs to the world. It is 'to eate the worlds due' just as the grave swallows us; it is in fact, as the closing phrase suggests, to be in league with the grave, to assist in what it is doing anyway. And with 'Pitty the world' the practical implications of the twice-used 'tender' are made explicit in a new context: as there exist mutual obligations of love between parent and child, so there is a relation between the individual and the world. *This* individual, at least, has a duty not to deprive it of its proper food.

It should be clear, then, what sort of questions the sonnet raises and in what terms the language puts them, what life it makes them live. The more one looks at this poetry the more one sees the real complexities which underlie the deceptively smooth surface.[1] In this it is a fitting start to a sequence where again and again the attentive reader must pause and ask, 'Just what is being said here? Is this affirmation or questioning? Or both, from different points of view?' In Sonnet I it is not just the equivocality of attitude which is characteristic of so many later sonnets: it is the slyness of tone which goes with this attitude and reveals it. The blade is sheathed in silk. Not praise alone, nor blame alone; not one and then the other; but both at once. And this is not a clever balancing-act or parrying of experience, nor an attempt to stand outside or above it: it is a recognition of many-sidedness, of the need to give full weight to the various and sometimes conflicting elements which may be

[1] Stephen Booth's book *An Essay on Shakespeare's Sonnets* deals at length with such complexities but it was published too late for me to take it into account in this study.

21

present simultaneously in human affairs. The result is an art which is, like life, difficult to read completely, an art which attends to the variousness of an experience and creates the equivalent of this in language. But Shakespeare is not simply noting or recording experience; his art is not merely mimetic, a secondary thing depending on mechanical fidelity to its subject-matter. On the contrary, it is freely creative, autonomous, and while its complex living patterns of meaning correspond with patterns of experience outside art, they exist here in their own order. If, in this sense, things happen here as they do in life, the poetry rarely compels attention to its significance by any striking gesture (mention of Donne should make this clear): the meaning or complex of meanings can be missed if one is too hurried to watch closely, to be attentively still. This is, as I shall argue later, a poetry born of 'negative capability', and it requires this gift in the reader also. To a remarkable extent it is a poetry for contemplation: it can be fully comprehended only by pondering line and phrase, turning them this way and that as they themselves turn. In this it strikingly resembles the poetry of *Four Quartets*, which likewise can be possessed only through a deep and contemplative listening of the whole being, and not less through an attentiveness to all the possibilities of individual words and phrases.

I should like to glance more quickly at the rest of the sonnets in this first group of seventeen. It is a critical commonplace that many of the Sonnets fall into groups which can be compared to the musical form of theme and variations.[1] This can certainly be said of Sonnets 1–17.[2] One

---

[1] See C.S. Lewis, *English Literature in the Sixteenth Century (Excluding Drama)* (Oxford, 1954), pp. 506–8; and J.B. Leishman entitles his book *Themes and Variations in Shakespeare's Sonnets* (London, 1961).

[2] The theme is derived from Erasmus through Wilson's *Arte of Rhetorique* (1553), where Shakespeare would have read the 'Epistle to persuade a

22

sonnet may amplify an idea from an earlier one; the next may extend it into a new area, a new aspect of the general concern; and throughout the set the main themes and images will be seen continually forming and re-forming in patterns like the dancers in a grave ballet.

While Sonnet 1 states the themes for the sonnets immediately following and also for the sequence at large, touching on the questions of what Time does to us and what we can do to resist him, it does this incompletely: the themes are announced, but they have still to be developed. The gradual unfolding, even naming, of various related aspects of the whole concern takes place in Sonnets 2–17, and by the time we have read them through we have been introduced to all the main subjects which will be discussed in the 126 sonnets addressed to the youth. They are questions which occur also in the sonnets to the mistress, but less directly and, of course, with the addition of others.

Murray Krieger remarks on

Shakespeare's brilliant method of creating constitutive symbols in one sonnet and, having earned his right to them there, transferring them whole to another sonnet, with their full burden of borrowed meaning, earned elsewhere, taken for granted. Thus a creative symbol in one sonnet becomes a sign, one of the raw materials, in another... The critic can treat the single poem as an aesthetic unit while still using it as an explicative instrument to reveal the interrelation among the sonnets that creates the oneness of their total symbolic system, their unified body of metaphor.[1]

Something like this happens in the tightly-organized group under discussion now. It is common to find a phrase or

young ientleman to Mariage, devised by Erasmus in the behalfe of his frende'. (Thomas Wilson, *The Arte of Rhetorique*, facsimile reproduction, ed. R.H. Bowers (Gainesville, 1962), pp. 54ff.)

[1] Murray Krieger, *A Window to Criticism: Shakespeare's Sonnets and Modern Poetics* (Princeton, 1964), p. 73.

image, used in one sonnet, repeated by a later one in a new context and so extended. Sometimes the earlier use is the establishing one and the meaning in the second case is largely borrowed from that; sometimes the new context throws a new light on the earlier image or even turns into an image what was merely a 'sign' before. Then, too, there may be repetition with little or no development, but used as a method of relating one phase of the total exploration of the theme to an earlier, and perhaps a later one. All of these seventeen poems have in common the one idea, that the youth must marry and have children. But they have more in common than that: they are related poetically, and in quite complex and intricate ways.

To give some examples. Sonnet 1 warns the youth not to '*eate* the worlds due, by the *grave* and thee'; in Sonnet 2 his continued singleness would be 'an *all-eating* shame'; in Sonnet 6 the 'eate' and 'grave' of 1 are echoed, if faintly, in 'To be deaths conquest and make wormes thine heire'. Again, 'beare his memory' from 1 is recalled at the end of 3: 'But if thou live remembred not to be', where 'remembred', according to Krieger's law, borrows the metaphoric force of the previous passage. To take a more complicated case, the 'wast in *niggarding*' of 1 is picked up in the 'beautious *nigard*' of 4, and this idea is extended throughout 4 in financial terms, which in turn receive a backward glance in 6: 'That use is not forbidden usery'. Again, notice the transition from Sonnet 2 to Sonnet 3:

> If thou couldst answere this faire child of mine
> Shall sum my count...

> Looke in thy glasse and tell the face thou vewest,
> Now is the time that face should forme an other.

In the first passage '*this* faire child' puts the child there, in an imagined situation, to be pointed out as his father's image. In the second the image is merely the one given back by the glass; yet, says the poet, there is a moral there too. These lines may at first seem to lack sharpness but on a closer reading they work quite subtly: the friend is to tell his mirrored face that that face, itself one kind of image, must create another, the face of a son. The mirror, then, is more than a mirror, it can also be a window. And indeed in Sonnet 3, 'glass' is made to change its meaning in just this way. The turning-point comes in lines 9–10:

> Thou art thy mothers glasse and she in thee
> Calls backe the lovely Aprill of her prime.

The poetry has progressed by stepping backwards in time. The friend is to his mother (the mirror image of her youth) what the poet would have a son be to the friend. 'Glasse' here still means mirror, though now the image is a living one and the gazer, rather than looking *into* the glass at the closed system of self and reflection, is almost looking *through* the glass: at another being, and one who recalls past youth. And so the modulation to the next two lines is achieved:

> So thou through windowes of thine age shalt see,
> Dispight of wrinkles this thy goulden time.

'Windowes', unlike mirrors, offer escape or at least a prospect of the larger world: solace for 'age' with its very physical 'wrinkles'.

Yet another example of imagery threading through a group of sonnets begins here in Sonnet 3 and carries us forward to 5 and 6. 'Glass', as well as meaning 'mirror' and 'window', can also mean a vessel, and Sonnet 5, after hinting noncommittally (in 'The lovely gaze where every eye doth dwell') at the first two, finally introduces the third;

but not before a new context of imagery has been formed, natural and seasonal, tactile as well as visual:

> For never resting time leads Summer on
> To hidious winter and confounds him there,
> Sap checkt with frost and lustie leav's quite gon.
> Beauty ore-snow'd and barenes every where.

After 'sap checkt with frost' in particular, we are prepared for the lines which follow:

> Then were not *summers distillation left*
> *A liquid prisoner pent in walls of glasse,*
> Beauties effect with beauty were bereft...
> > But *flowers distil'd* though they with winter meete,
> > Leese but their show, their substance still lives sweet.

The next sonnet carries this on and unites it with a suggestion from Sonnet 3, the poet's fear lest the friend 'beguile the world, unblesse some mother'. After that, 'make sweet some *viall*' in 6 suggests both the child and the woman who bears him.

And again, what is said of 'hidious winter' in 5 is condensed by 6 in the opening metaphor of 'winters wragged hand' and expanded by much of the imagery of 12 and by the reference in 13 to 'the stormy gusts of winters day / And barren rage of deaths eternall cold'. It is clear that the concerted effect of these passages is to build an impression of winter and of the destruction it represents. Indeed, the whole pattern of repetition and extension throughout these sonnets forms a rich carpet of suggestion, a texture of reiterated but varied persuasion. There are, too, interruptions of this pattern which further elaborate the whole design: poems like 4, 7 and 14 which confine themselves to working out a single conceit and play little part in the give-and-take with other sonnets.

Three other features of the group should be noticed. One

is the poet's attitude, which begins by being completely self-effacing, and, in fact, remains largely so; it is not until the end of Sonnet 10 that he makes any claim for a relationship between himself and the youth, and then it is far from strong: 'Make thee an other selfe *for love of me*'. The poet's sense of the youth's value is everywhere apparent before and after this, but it is conveyed with tact, with a servant's remoteness. Only in this couplet and in the couplet of 13 is there any approach to greater intimacy:

> O none but unthrifts, *deare my love* you know,
> You had a Father, let your Son say so.

The point is, however, that the closer relationship seen in later sonnets (18–126) is already foreshadowed here, like so much else.

Secondly, the general imaginative movement in this first group is an expansive one. This seems to be involuntary as well as deliberate. While Sonnet 1 seems to know quite certainly what it is doing, one may feel that the sequence steadily moves outward in sonnet after sonnet to a wider awareness of what was implied in that starting-point. The increasing exploration of the human themes in natural and seasonal terms is one sign that Shakespeare's imagination is broadening and deepening the range of meanings hinted at in the opening sonnet.

Thirdly, it is here that poetry is first mentioned and its role asserted. The group considers not one but two means of transcending time and death, in a gradual discovery of new corridors of possibility. Sonnet 12 ends:

> And nothing gainst Times sieth can make defence
> Save breed to brave him, when he takes thee hence.

But later poems in the group qualify that: they speak of that other form of imitation with which the poet is by his nature concerned. The way has been prepared for this by the mirror, window and vial metaphors already discussed. From the 'image' in the mirror, the 'flowers distil'd', it is no distance to art seen as a means of distilling beauty and defeating time. The image of art as a distilling is seldom prominently used later, but it underlies quite naturally all the assertions that poetry will immortalize the beloved. For the present the claims are fairly modest ones; certainly they are weighed against others. Sonnet 15 ends:

> And all in war with Time for love of you
> As he takes from you, I ingraft you new.

And in the manner already established, this theme is developed through the rest of the group and is carried over the bridge formed by Sonnet 18 into the larger sequence. Sonnet 16 refers slightingly to the poet's 'barren rime', 17 to the disbelief with which that 'rime' may meet:

> And your true rights be termed a Poets rage,
> And stretched miter of an Antique song.

18, more hopefully, speaks of 'eternall lines':

> So long as men can breath or eyes can see,
> So long lives this, and this gives life to thee.

In the couplet of 15, the image, with overtones of Saint Paul, is of a new life created by grafting that of the beloved into language; *this* posterity at least, for what it is worth, the poet can promise. But the next sonnet immediately puts it in perspective:

> But wherefore do not you a mightier waie
> Make warre uppon this bloudie tirant time?
> And fortifie your selfe in your decay
> With meanes more blessed then my barren rime?

Here and elsewhere the poet who speaks in the Sonnets is

28

fully prepared to admit the limitations of his power. Presumably he would have agreed with D.H. Lawrence's remark that *lives* were more important than anything else, even works of art; and one remembers G. Wilson Knight's remarks about 'breath' in his discussion of the statue scene in *The Winter's Tale*. Commenting on Leontes' 'What fine chisel/Could ever yet cut breath', he says: 'However highly we value the eternity phrased by art (as in Yeats' "monuments of unaging intellect" in *Sailing to Byzantium* and Keats' *Grecian Urn*), yet there is a frontier beyond which it and all corresponding philosophies fail: they lack one thing, breath. With a fine pungency of phrase...a whole world of human idealism is dismissed.'[1] The same realization is clear in the Shakespeare of the Sonnets: he sees that selves, persons, are the ultimate goals of love: who in his senses would prefer a poem to his friend's living child? It is in this context that 'rime' may seem 'barren', 'poor', a 'stretched metre'. The poet's estimate of his poetry is generally marked by humility, or perhaps we should say realism. I must return to this later in discussing the greater sonnets on the power of art, but for the moment his attitude is best summed up in the couplet of Sonnet 17:

> But were some childe of yours alive that time,
> You should live twise, in it and in my rime,[2]

This discussion of the first seventeen sonnets should have shown some features of the poetry we find in later sonnets as well: above all, the workings of the language to create a delicate, unobtrusive richness of texture. If this is to be found in the early sonnets, it is all the more evident in the later ones. So far the poetry has been comparatively simple

---

[1] G. Wilson Knight, *The Crown of Life* (London, 1965), p. 123.
[2] I have amended the punctuation of the Quarto in this line.

and direct, like the argument it embodies. For these seven-teen sonnets meet the youth's narcissism with a relatively simple response, neatly summed up in a line from Sonnet 16: 'To give away your selfe, keeps your selfe still'. Many later sonnets, though by no means rejecting this advice, are much more searching. The attitudes, and the poetry along with them, become more complex, more difficult to calculate, and never more so than in the poem I want to examine now.

Sonnet 94

Though the difficulties of this poem are very generally recognized, it is surprising how few critics have tried to unravel them. Empson's virtuoso performance[1] is deservedly well known, but in the years since it appeared there have been few sustained attempts to follow it up.[2] The tendency has been to acknowledge that the poem is difficult, and this discussion of it brilliant, and then to pass on. But the brilliance is dazzling as well as illuminating, and with all gratitude to Empson one may feel the need to go back to the sonnet and with his help ponder it again. Certainly, in any discussion of what the Sonnets say about self-love, it has to be examined with some care.

> They that have powre to hurt, and will doe none,
> That doe not do the thing, they most do showe,
> Who moving others, are themselves as stone,
> Unmooved, could, and to temptation slow:
> They rightly do inherrit heavens graces,
> And husband natures ritches from expence,

[1] 'They that have power' (1935) in *Some Versions of Pastoral*, pp. 75–96.
[2] Apart from L.C. Knights (1934) who precedes Empson, perhaps the most helpful critics of this sonnet are: Patrick Cruttwell, *The Shake-spearean Moment* (New York, 1960), pp. 30–1; M.M. Mahood, *Shake-speare's Wordplay* (London, 1957), pp. 98–100; Hilton Landry, *Interpreta-tions in Shakespeare's Sonnets* (Berkeley and Los Angeles, 1963), pp. 7–27; J.W. Lever, *The Elizabethan Love Sonnet* (London, 1966), pp. 209–21.

> They are the Lords and owners of their faces,
> Others, but stewards of their excellence:
> The sommers flowre is to the sommer sweet,
> Though to it selfe, it onely live and die,
> But if that flowre with base infection meete,
> The basest weed out-braves his dignity:
>> For sweetest things turne sowrest by their deedes,
>> Lillies that fester, smell far worse then weeds.

'It is agreed', says Empson, 'that *They that have power to hurt and will do none* is a piece of grave irony'; but suppose it is not agreed? I am sure Empson is right; but let us try to read the poem as if it were devoid of irony and see what sense it makes.

Those who have power to hurt and will not use it, who do not do what they most seem to do (or be, or represent), who while they move others are themselves like stone, un-moved, cold, slow to temptation: they, justly and by right, possess heaven's grace, and conserve the riches of nature (which could be their own natural gifts or the goods showered upon them), seeing to it that these are not squandered. Such men are the true aristocrats, the lords and land-lords. They are also the lords of their faces, that is, of what they appear to be; and not only the lords but the *owners* of their faces; which means, perhaps, that they own (acknowledge) their faces as the reality. And since these are the lords and owners, others are only stewards of their excellence; stewards, presumably, of the lords' excellence (with over-tones, noted by Empson, of the stewards' form of address, 'Their Excellencies', and of their admiration and perhaps the poet's as well). Now comes, it would seem, a sudden break in the thought: the summer's flower is sweet to the summer although the flower itself is conscious of merely living and dying. The going becomes harder here, for another reading suggests itself: to the summer the flower is sweet, but the flower itself is concerned only with living and dying, it is indifferent to its effect on others and to their feelings. Moreover the flower is the summer's flower, so the summer as well as finding it sweet has produced it. The flower therefore, simply living and dying to itself, apparently gives its debt to the summer (for admiration, for existence) no thought at all. And of course, beyond and before all this, 'onely' ('one-ly') means 'singly', and points to the infertility of the flower: it neither gives nor receives new life, and we are reminded of the things said about the singleness of the youth in the first seventeen sonnets. The transition to the next two lines appears difficult at first and might best be managed by temporarily treating the line 'Though to it selfe, it onely live and die' as parenthetical. The thought then runs: The summer's flower is sweet to the summer, but if it meet with base infection, if it should become corrupted, the merest weed (which has perhaps corrupted it: 'base... basest'?) not only survives it but, lowly as it is, seems to fare better. For sweetest things turn sourest by their deeds, and the deeds of *this* flower are now to fester and to stink: better a weed's smell than that of a rotting lily.

This reading makes some sense of the poem, and looks the more persuasive for taking some account of ambiguities in word and phrase. But too many major difficulties are passed over. The chief of these is the question of tone; but, to leave that aside for the moment, the reading comes dangerously close to admitting irony as soon as it reaches the sestet. What one finds here, in connection with the flower, is irony of sense as distinct from irony conveyed by tone: the different possibilities held out by the language, especially in the phrase 'to it selfe'. And since nothing in the poem seems to rule out any of these, one may presume that all are valid – and intentional. And if the flower lives and dies to itself, without acknowledging what it owes to the summer, are we to think this laudable? There is certainly a jump in the thought between octave and sestet, and a more violent one than is usual in the Sonnets, but not a break. Though the imagery changes, the preoccupation (not to mention the tone) remains the same. Further, the later images take their pattern from the earlier: lords and stewards become flower and summer, flower and weed. The feudal relationship is replaced by natural relationships, but these are seen partly in hierarchical terms. So that even on the level of images the two sections of the poem are connected. The first two lines of the sestet look deceptively simple, and I am probably not the only reader to have carried them away singing in his head but to have had no idea of their function in the poem as a whole. In context, just *because* they seem so innocent, they may bring us up short: after the earlier complications their very ease may make us uneasy. And the ambiguities (already considered) in these two lines are enough to make it seem pretty certain that irony is present after all.

To recognize this is to find new freedom and scope, if also more problems. Which parts are ironical and which are not, or is the poem ironical from start to finish? And (whatever the answer to this) how far are the ironies to be carried? The main freedom gained, of course, is to be able to consider the sonnet's tone. The lines about the flower cast a questioning light on all the previous lines, but even in themselves they throw up questions ignored by the earlier approach. While it seems thoroughly praiseworthy that 'they' who have the power to hurt should lack the will to exercise it, one is slightly unsettled by the next line: they *appear* to be the sort of people who would do something (whatever it is), yet they don't do it. From the first line to the second there is a swift and puzzling change in the direction of the thought. In the first, 'they' are said to refrain from *hurting*; in the second, the emphasis has shifted from their 'power' to their 'show': and the word has presumably its usual Shakespearean connotations. It is hard to suppose, despite the impression given by the syntax, that line 2 is saying the same thing as line 1; it may indeed be talking about the obverse of what line 1, apparently, points to. 'Apparently', for perhaps that line has some of the slyness of tone we find in so many of the Sonnets. 'They have power, and power to hurt, but will not use it to that end': one must, in general, admire that; but are they equally to be admired for not doing what 'they most do showe'? Whatever (once again) that may be: for while it could be the power to hurt, this seems unlikely. The poetry is already moving too purposefully for this line to be merely an empty parallel to the first. We are never told in precise terms what 'the thing' is (perhaps it is a range of different but related things found in different but related cases), but everything said about 'them' here and further on is in negative terms: 'moving others, [they] are themselves as stone,/Unmooved, could, and to temptation slow'. Such dispositions hardly excite praise; they are not even as tolerable as those of the Petrarchan mistress, which they call to mind. She too moved others while remaining herself as stone, but 'slow to temptation' would have been felt too strong a charge. It suggests a different kind of character, one with a greater moral dimension for one thing: the Petrarchan mistress tempted others without, as a rule, being tempted herself. (Sidney's Stella is of course an exception to this rule.) Yet, like the Petrarchan mistress again, Shakespeare's people are compared to the lodestone,

34

the image of 'moving others... themselves as stone, un-moved' having a double force: (1) the hearts of others are stirred, 'theirs' remain unmoved, 'cold as any stone'; (2) others are drawn to them as metal to the magnet, 'they' like the magnet remain motionless. (Looking more closely still for a moment at '[they] are themselves as stone', one notices how the phrase, when dwelt upon, acquires a shape similar to that of a sentence like 'He was himself as Hamlet'. They are themselves as stone, stone expresses their nature: the more they are like stone, the more fully they are them-selves.)

The thought of the quatrain develops in such a way that the end seems almost to reverse the beginning. After the fourth line, it would hardly be a surprise to go back and find that the first read 'They that have powre to *heal*, and will doe none'. And after such a fourth line the tone of the fifth has to be ironical. The ambiguity of 'rightly', noted before, remains. On the one hand the word means 'as of right', and taken with 'inherit' and 'heavens graces' has suggestions of nobility, even of kingship; on the other hand it appears to express approval, though this approval turns out to be apparent only. Both meanings need to be caught if we are not to miss the doubleness of the poem's statement. In a sense these people do 'rightly' (indeed and by right) inherit heaven's graces: every blessing and favour (includ-ing that of being well-favoured?) they possess by inheri-tance. Yet perhaps every man receives as much? Why then should *these* think themselves exceptional? But perhaps they *have* received greater gifts, or gifts in greater measure? They were perhaps born rich, in whatever sense: clearly then their riches are theirs by right. No irony so far; but, given what has already been said of them, do they act *justly*? The rightful heirs may not 'do what's right'. And the phrase

'heavens graces' could be irony of the type which con-
demns a man's attitude by representing it ('Of course,
you're never wrong'). 'They' are perhaps too much inclined to take their gifts for granted, to lack a sense of
noblesse oblige. Certainly all this is supported by the lines
before and after. The relation between 'heavens graces' and
'natures ritches' may not be altogether clear: are they the
same thing, or are they complementary, or opposed? No
clear indication is given. The notion of husbanding nature's
riches looks straightforward enough but the next phrase
adroitly upsets it: 'And husband natures ritches *from expence*'. Taken one way (the primary one, I think), this could
mean, as suggested before, that they cultivate and conserve
the riches of nature, and prevent them from being wasted.
But it could also mean that they hoard these riches and
prevent them from being used at all. This supposes that
both the use and the riches are in the hands of those who
have power. Alternatively, the line may attribute the hoard-
ing to them and the expense to others; they hoard what
others spend, or they reap the fruits of other men's labours,
or both. Thus the relation between 'heavens graces' (which
are 'theirs') and 'natures ritches' (which are others') becomes clearer. 'They' believe themselves to be, and doubt-
less are, graced by heaven, and lord it over the natural
world and the common people alike, while owning no
obligation to spend on anyone the riches of their own
natures.

The strongly ironic note may sound more subdued in the
next line: they are (whatever else) the 'Lords and owners'
of *something*. Lords *and* owners: the first word gets a capital
in order, probably, to emphasize their rank and the homage
paid to them, while the two words together mark the twin
attributes of rank and proprietorship. The second word,

moreover, forms a bridge to the next line, stressing the gulf which separates a mere steward from a lord – though of course there was a relationship as well, which Shakespeare's age knew both as a social fact and from the Bible. The parables of lords and servants, and particularly that of the talents, the parable of the pharisee and the publican, even, I think, the parable of the marriage feast: largely by appeal to these, and to the familiar moral attitudes they embody, the reader's judgment is being shaped. In the parables the lord is owner of slaves, lands, cattle, vineyards. What do these lords own? Their faces. When read in one way, the line swells and collapses with an almost comic effect, as L. C. Knights has observed.[1] And while the face may identify a person, may possess a beauty which dazzles others, as many of the Sonnets tell us the youth's face does, it may also of course be a mere façade; one recalls the familiar Shakespearean contrast between appearance and inward state: 'There's no art/To find the mind's construction in the face'; 'I have that within which passeth show'. And 'show', of course, is mentioned in the sonnet itself. There is, too, I think, a further whisper of irony: just as the lords are owners of their *faces*, so the stewards are busy about *excellence*, not lands or goods but an abstract thing; which fits in with all that the poem says about *not doing*.

These two lines can be read another way, however: the 'excellence' of the second line may be that of the stewards. The first kind of people, though not necessarily like the pharisees in hypocrisy, are like them in hollowness; they are 'big' and they know it, and this 'knowledge' loses them the laurels they rest on. 'They have their reward already': face, pomp, empty show. Others are humble enough to

[1] L. C. Knights, 'Shakespeare's Sonnets' in *Explorations* (Harmondsworth, 1964), p. 64.

make themselves stewards of the talents given them – excellent to begin with, but improved by industry. One can speak of 'their excellence', though this of course would never occur to *them*.

> The sommers flowre is to the sommer sweet,
> Though to it selfe, it onely live and die,
> But if that flowre with base infection meete,
> The basest weed out-braves his dignity:

I have suggested that the flower may take corruption from the weed, but this need not be so, and nothing depends on it: it is only one of the many possibilities thrown up by the extraordinary suggestiveness of the language. Beautiful but passive (and it may be helpful to remember Yeats on the decline of ancestral houses), the aristocratic flower becomes so debased by infection that even the 'basest weed' has the advantage, can 'outbrave' the flower's 'dignity', which by implication is now almost nothing: *corruptio optimi pessima*. What does the far-from-strong verb 'meete' convey? Is it merely neutral: 'if the flower becomes infected'? Not quite, though on the other hand 'meete' doesn't suggest anything so positive as an embrace; and to meet with an accident is not necessarily to be accident-prone. All the same, just because the word is such an open one and takes colour from its context, it leads one to suspect that the flower, through too much passivity, lets the infection in.

One further point needs to be made concerning the final couplet. The equivocality of 'sweetest things turne sowrest by their deedes' depends upon a double-take on the last word. The 'deedes' are not initially those of festering and smelling: that can only be said of the flowers in their last state, but their first, as the whole poem has shown, was one of inaction. They have done nothing, their 'deedes' were non-deeds; in Pound's words, 'Here error is all in the not-done'. And yet these too, like vigorous action, have their consequences: see the last line, which, one may note, is the simplest in the poem. It needs to be, because, coming at the end of such a sequence of ironic ambiguities, it has to strike an unequivocal hammer-blow. It contains no irony: it needs none.

* * *

'A piece of grave irony'. I have said something of the ironies, little or nothing of what might be meant by 'grave'. But the poem's gravity of manner and of preoccupation is probably clear enough, and the ironies in no way conflict with this: indeed, they not only fortify the gravity, they are the marrow of its bones.

Despite what has been said, the poem remains, in some ways, cryptic and unexplained. If, as I have done so far, we consider it in isolation from the rest of the Sonnets, it must give very strongly the impression of being a 'reference to an undiscovered plot'. Precisely what happenings prompted the poem? For it is hard not to think that it refers to actual events it does not specify. Martin Seymour-Smith explains (pp. 158–9) that it forms part of a sequence (Sonnets 87–96) dealing with the friend's desire to leave Shakespeare and his unwillingness to say so. Seymour-Smith's mistake is not in finding a 'story-line' in these sonnets but in thinking that it explains all the difficulties. Some, however, are a matter of Shakespeare's deeper preoccupations, and of their change and development from sonnet to sonnet. Sonnet 94 can't be fully explained by pointing to 92, 'But doe thy worst to steale thy selfe away', though this and all the sonnets from 88 to 93 do contemplate the friend's possible desertion. Whatever 94 is about, it is not simply about that. Rather, it seems to belong to a smaller group of five poems

(92–6) concerned with a hidden fault. A key line or two from the others will show this:

> But whats so blessed faire that feares no blot,
> Thou maist be falce, and yet I know it not. (92)

> So shall I live, supposing thou art true. (93)

> How sweet and lovely dost thou make the shame...
> Oh in what sweets doest thou thy sinnes inclose! (95)

> Some say thy fault is youth, some wantonesse. (96)

Of all these, the sonnets immediately before and after 94 are the most help. 95 takes from 94 the idea of the beautiful but cankered flower, but puts it to different and less subtle uses. 93, however, is a genuine preparation for the sonnet that follows it.

> So shall I live, supposing thou art true,
> Like a deceived husband, so loves face,
> May still seeme love to me, though alter'd new:
> Thy lookes with me, thy heart in other place.
> For their can live no hatred in thine eye,
> Therefore in that I cannot know thy change,
> In manies lookes, the falce hearts history
> Is writ in moods and frounes and wrinckles strange.
> But heaven in thy creation did decree,
> That in thy face sweet love should ever dwell,
> What ere thy thoughts, or thy hearts workings be,
> Thy lookes should nothing thence, but sweetnesse tell.
>   How like *Eaves* apple doth thy beauty grow,
>   If thy sweet vertue answere not thy show.

This defines a situation and (more important) brings forward ideas and key words which the next poem shares. Sonnet 93, in fact, is almost entirely about the contrast between hearts and faces: the face *versus* the heart's workings, sweetness and virtue *versus* show. But in 94 these materials have not only been transmuted, they have been compounded with others, to produce something strange as well as rich. Without becoming abstract the poetry is more generalized, more lofty, more compressed. Much more is happening: we recognize that, even if we know that some of it eludes us. And if it does so, it is not so much because the *events* referred to are not stated as because the poet's concerns have become so much deeper and more complex.

But if the poem partly eludes us, this may not be entirely our fault. It is not to deny the poem's great power and stature to say that, as in some of the other sonnets (for example, 60, 'Like as the waves...'), Shakespeare has possibly tried to say too much in one sonnet. With the exception of the word 'hurt', which does, I think, look beyond the poem, a fairly coherent, fairly inclusive account of the poem's meaning, or meanings, can be given, but only after a most strenuous battle with the compressed and rapidly shifting language. Perhaps it is beside the point to ask if Shakespeare has expected too much of his reader: he may well have written this sonnet for a very select audience, possibly for himself alone.

On the other hand, this critical line of thought seems almost trifling when one considers how much the poem (whatever its private purpose) communicates to us, readers not of the poet's circle; how suggestive it is of the ironies and ambiguities of its subject. It is in fact one of the most rewarding of all the sonnets on the deceptions and sterility of self-love, one of the most profoundly searching meditations on a beauty more of show than of substance: how like Eve's apple, deceitfully beautiful yet still fascinating even to the man who has already guessed what it conceals. For, of course, the poem is anything but a detached judgment of a certain type of person. Someone has had the power to hurt;

the poet is deeply involved, as his generalization, 'They that have powre', tells us. It is like that of Wyatt in 'They fle from me': Wyatt too says 'they', but he means above all the *she* whose loose gown fell from her shoulders and who caught him in her 'armes long and small'. In each case the plural is, partly at least, a resort from an all-too-particular instance, too close and too painful to be expressed in the singular. There are differences too, of course. For Wyatt, the generalization is really a way *into* the particular memory, a bearable means of approach. For Shakespeare, the movement is, rather, *away* from the central experience; it is never forgotten or lost, but the poem broods upon it, enlarges upon it, until it becomes a general experience as well as a particular one. By universalizing it in this way, Shakespeare escapes from the limitations of the self. It would have been easy to fall into self-pity or mere denunciation, both traps in which the poet, and the friend with him, would rapidly shrink to pygmy size. But while the experience, the relationship, is kept in sight, Shakespeare's mind moves from the plane of 'I' and 'thou' towards a more expansive region of the imagination, where the friend is seen both as himself and as a particularly striking example of a whole order of beings who act on those about them in a certain way. The purpose of the generalization is ultimately not that of self-protection for the poet, nor evasion of any problem which his relationship with the youth has throw up for him: instead it is a means of transcending the limited self for both of them. This is the way some people behave, the poem is saying, the way some people are made: you are one of them, and I am one of those whom they can hurt. But the poem is not saying, *Che sera, sera*. Here, characteristically, Shakespeare refuses the stoical or fatalistic way out, as the tone, the imagery, the whole complex life of the poetry shows beyond question. It offers nothing so crude as a warning, though it contains an element of something like one; neither does it show a defeated assent to whatever people, or fortune, may hand out. The poet has not been morally cowed. On the contrary, his attitude, with its extraordinary balance between angry, loving, temperate condemnation and ironic and therefore dignified acceptance, is a moral triumph as well as an imaginative one.

2

Sin of Self-Love: the Poet

─────

In Sonnet 94 the attitude is ambivalent: if there is condemnation there is also love, and, for many readers, more than a hint of envy as well.[1] The ambivalence derives, of course, from the fact that the poet is looking at a disturbing trait in another: someone, moreover, whom he loves and has admired. When he turns his gaze upon himself one can expect different results. It is one thing to see self-centredness in someone you love, another to recognize it in yourself. The sonnets which embody this recognition are to be found in both the group to the youth and the group to the mistress. One or other of these figures may be mentioned or implied in the poem, but its main concern is with the poet's own conscience. The strain put upon that conscience is greatest, of course, in the relationship with the mistress; Patrick Cruttwell finds in the poet here 'an utter disintegration of the personality'.[2] That is not quite accurate: even here he goes on confronting himself with the truth, even when he would prefer to be deceived. He may want to give up the truth but he cannot succeed for long: it will not give him up.

But well before we come to that relationship, the self-examination begins.

─────

[1] Both William Empson and Patrick Cruttwell point to this.
[2] *The Shakespearean Moment*, p. 12.

44

Sonnet 62

Sinne of self-love possesseth al mine eie,
And all my soule, and al my every part;
And for this sinne there is no remedie,
It is so grounded inward in my heart.
Me thinkes no face so gratious is as mine,
No shape so true, no truth of such account,
And for my selfe mine owne worth do define,
As I all other in all worths surmount.
But when my glasse shewes me my selfe indeed
Beated and chopt with tand antiquitie,
Mine owne selfe love quite contrary I read:
Selfe, so selfe loving were iniquity,
　　T'is thee (my selfe) that for my selfe I praise,
　　Painting my age with beauty of thy daies.

Compared to 'They that have powre', this sonnet may well seem something of an anticlimax. It is less striking, less enigmatically challenging, less rich in its language. Yet it is one of the central poems in the whole sequence and focuses some of its main preoccupations: the poet's love for the friend, his awareness of age, and above all, the concern with self-love which we are now pursuing. It is obviously related to the sonnets already discussed, but now narcissism is to be seen in the poet himself, and he deals more harshly, certainly more bluntly, with the 'iniquity' of the state than he did in Sonnets 1–17. Self-love, which possesses poet and friend alike, each in his fashion, must now be faced at still closer range.

As Martin Seymour-Smith remarks (p. 144), 'It is not the self-love itself which obsesses him, but the sin, and the guilty need for it'; and as the octave shows, this is a sin of the imagination: the poet is 'clouded with his own conceit', it possesses 'all his eye', but this is the inward eye (that bliss of solitude). Such a conceit, as the sestet will prove, is begotten in absence from his mirror, and, with the sin, is 'grounded inward' in his heart, a radical flaw for which 'there is no remedie'. In the second quatrain the gaze is still inward: 'Me *thinkes* no face so gratious is as mine'. This 'dream of himself' swells as the quatrain proceeds (with a pun on 'true': well-proportioned as well as embodying or conforming to the truth), until the dream is, *he* is, the measure of all things, and his worth surpasses all other worths. The verbal sequence with its interlinking threads, 'no face so gratious...no shape so true...no truth of such account', together with the closely-knit syntax of the next two lines and the culmination and settling of the whole verbal movement in the final word 'surmount': these form the exact equivalent of the sequence of the poet's thoughts in their rapid climb to the supreme delusion.

From which, the sharp descent: a glance in the mirror dispels the dream, and there is nothing of 'through a glass darkly' about this picture. 'But when my glasse shewes me my selfe indeed': the heavy stress on 'shewes', after several metrically regular lines, stresses the jolt from illusion into reality. The poet may *fancy* what he likes; his glass *shows* him the truth. Nor is it the face alone he sees 'Beated and chopt with tand antiquitie', for the face shows, and is, the self indeed; and to love this self, as he does, is plainly 'iniquity'.

But the couplet suggests a possible redemption. The beloved is the poet's better self, is more himself than *he* is, in particular because, besides being loved as the poet loves himself, he is young and beautiful: he is as the poet wishes to see himself and, thanks to his glass, cannot; and so the beloved might make satisfaction for the poet's 'sin', might indeed release him from it. There is more than one mirror in the poem: the second is the friend ('thee (my selfe)') who throws back to the poet an image that corrects all imperfection. He is beautiful in himself, he is loved by the poet *as* himself, he is the image of the poet as the poet would like to be. And by being other, perhaps he can enable the poet to overcome his sin. A substitution is possible, the poet claims. He need no longer love his own false picture of himself: *instead of himself* and *for his own sake* (the double force of '*for* my selfe' in line 13), he can repair his own ugliness with the beauty of the beloved, his other self.

Such is the claim, but do we find it convincing? Martin Seymour-Smith does not: the sonnet, he says, 'peters out into the conceit of the identity of his [the poet's] "self" with the Friend' (p. 144). Certainly, after the rich equivocations of 'They that have powre', this sonnet seems slighter, less conscious of what it is doing and of the ambiguous ground it treads, especially towards its close. Does this close offer a deliberate irony or is it just one of the weak couplets we meet in a number of the Sonnets? It is difficult to know. Not only is the verbal design of the first twelve lines firm and accomplished, but certain touches in the couplet itself are reassuring, in particular the ambiguity of 'for', already noted: I love you instead of myself for my own sake. This appears to be intentional: not only is it the sort of sly word-play habitual with Shakespeare, but it is of a piece with the language of the rest of the poem. It seems as if the poet is aware that to praise another for oneself may well be to tread a quicksand: self-love cannot really be transmuted or escaped. The juxtaposition of 'my age' and 'beauty of thy daies' (linked by that usually pejorative word 'painting') is perhaps prompting the question: Can it be done? Can the bud renew the withered branch? Perhaps the conceit of the last line is offered as being no more than a 'receipt for deceit'? To take a different point: the friend is the poet's mirror, but the poet is now confessing to a sin which he has already found in the friend. Does the friend, then, indeed mirror the poet: beauty exchanged for ugliness, but self-regard answering self-regard; the same sin, despite the fair face, reflected back unchanged?

The question is whether these subtleties are really part of the poetic purpose and effect. The couplet does, I think, feel a bit glib, and on its own it lacks the resources needed to give enough imaginative force to the idea that the beloved is a second self. On the other hand we can find a number of other sonnets which suggest that at the end of 62 the poet might well know how insecure his solution is. But this raises the further question: Should other sonnets be got in to help this one stand up? Speaking generally we may say that each sonnet in the sequence is final and yet *not* final, that some sonnets (such as 'Let me not to the marriage of true mindes') can be read apart from the rest with neither gain nor loss, and that a large number, as it were *provisionally* self-sufficient, are modified or heightened by others, whether in close proximity or not, and perhaps by the sequence as a whole. But these considerations, obvious enough to most readers of the sequence, are not much help in reaching a decision about this sonnet. Does Shakespeare intend the weakness of the couplet: is he deliberately showing the lover's comforting self-delusion, or is he falling into it himself? I am inclined to think the latter. The way out of the poet's predicament is proffered in too smooth and facile a manner, and we have to work hard to persuade ourselves that the verse is really pointing us to the flaws we can find in the project.

Yet one may feel that in this sonnet as in others a good deal is achieved, and is not to be undone by a facile ending. The opening of the sestet, above all, offers a powerfully

realized image for the facts which the poet must acknowledge in himself: 'Beated and chopt with tand antiquitie'.
Hardly flattering: and this is what the poet must confront
in the mirror. The three adjectives work closely into a
strong and individual impression, at once visual and tactile,
associating the man with less than human things. Fallow
land cut and burnt off for manure; a surface furrowed and
criss-crossed by wear or weather; a hide toughened and
darkened by the tanning process: from these unlovely
objects we can infer what it is to grow old and know it.
(Though it must be added that there is nothing diseased or
disgusting about any of these: they all belong to a world of
things undergoing the processes to which nature or man
must put them.)

Sonnet 62, though not completely satisfying, is 'essential
reading' among the Sonnets: it occupies a central position
among the realities with which they deal, and points to one
of the most important dimensions of Shakespeare's awareness of love and of the self. And even if we read it partly in
the light of sonnets elsewhere in the sequence, it too illumi-
nates others, and by carrying the attack into the poet's own
camp, shows all the more clearly the futility and vacuity of
self-regard.

Sonnet 138

When my love sweares that she is made of truth,
I do beleeve her though I know she lyes,
That she might thinke me some untuterd youth,
Unlearned in the worlds false subtilties.
Thus vainely thinking that she thinkes me young,
Although she knowes my dayes are past the best,
Simply I credit her false speaking tongue,
On both sides thus is simple truth supprest:
But wherefore sayes she not she is unjust?

And wherefore say not I that I am old?
O loves best habit is in seeming trust,
And age in love, loves not t'have yeares told.
  Therefore I lye with her, and she with me,
  And in our faults by lyes we flattered be.

This, too, seems to me an 'examination of conscience'.
Here, in the relationship with the mistress, the poet recognizes his acquiescence in falsehood of thought or conduct –
though like C.L. Barber I am surprised to find Patrick
Cruttwell (pp. 13–14) describing this as 'perhaps the most
terrible poem of the whole sequence [to the mistress]...
the most terrible, and also the nakedest, since it confesses
things that are not easily confessed'; and equally surprised
when he goes on to talk of the 'grim seriousness' of the pun
on 'lye'. Barber is surely right to modify this: ' "Grim"
seems to me wrong: I find the poem jaunty as well as
devastating, and more honest so.' ('An Essay on the Sonnets', pp. 28–9.) There *are* grim poems to the woman, some
of which I shall consider shortly: she, it seems, provoked the
great outburst against 'Th'expence of Spirit in a waste of
shame'; but 138 is not one of these. We need only put it
beside 'Th'expence of Spirit' to see this. It is cooler and
more polished; it is in fact an extremely elegant poem (I
like Dr Barber's word 'jaunty', provided that it doesn't
obscure this elegance), and its particular kind of verbal play
provides the key to the poet's attitude. His knowledge of
the lying, on both sides, is recognized, admitted, acquiesced
in: the graceful, punning, shrugging manner tempers the
knowledge (in both senses of the word), and the restraint
masters, while it reveals, the trouble of the poet's mind.
The sonnet is remarkable for the tightly-knit movement of
the verse from quatrain to quatrain to final couplet. Whatever may be the case with other sonnets, the full stops and

colon here do not break the poem's development: rather, they mark its stages. (Contrast the form of this sonnet with, for example, that of 73, 'That time of yeeare thou maist in me behold', where the quatrains do not so much develop as reinforce each other by moving in parallel.)

The intricate pattern of mutual deception is established by the language of the first two lines:

> When my love sweares/that she is made of truth,
> I do beleeve her/though I know she lyes.

And there is a feeling of to-and-fro, of proposition and answer in the syntactical movement and in the rise and fall of the verse. There are perhaps two puns:

> *made* of truth,
> *maid* of truth.

> I know she *lyes*: to me
> I know she *lyes*: with others.

As so often happens in the Sonnets, these two lines, complete in themselves, form part of a larger whole and are extended by the two lines following.

> I do beleeve her though I know she lyes,
> That she might thinke me some untutered youth.

The sequence, as in many poems which concern doubleness of situation or of attitude, points to this doubleness by its very language-patterns. The two halves of line 2 may each be taken in turn with line 3. The first, and primary, meaning is: 'I do beleeve her/That she might thinke me some untuterd youth', and immediately the sense of 'beleeve' is seen to have altered. For line 2 by itself appeared to mean: Although I know she is lying, I believe her (because I choose to). Now, taken with the following line, 'I do beleeve her' has become a piece of indirect speech: I feign belief *so that* she will think me some untutored youth. The second alternative, 'I know she lyes/That she might thinke me some untuterd youth', means: She lies to deceive me, to find me (so deceived) a mere untutored youth, and therefore at a disadvantage. The combined effect of these ambiguities is to re-create a situation in which both partners are lying and being deceived: and, in the man's case at least, willingly so. Passing to line 4, one might at first think it is there merely to fill out the quatrain. 'Unlearned' adds little to 'untuterd', though it does bring us a step closer to 'subtilties', which are for the learned rather than the merely taught. The unwary might suppose that in 'the worlds false subtilties' the only word that is really working is the last. But the line mentions *false* subtleties because subtleties are not always false (as the poet shows by his subtle awareness of the truth of all this falsehood, his own included), and because while the woman thinks she is being subtle the man realizes the truths behind her falsehoods. And if we take the phrase as a whole, and the rest of the two-line clause it helps to form, we get, once more, both her point of view and (secondarily this time) his:

I 'believe' her:

1. That she might think: This is a mere youth who knows nothing of the subtleties of ' the world' (as he would call it), nothing of people like me, or of the deceptions we practise; and who may draw aside prudishly from 'worldly' corruption.

2. That she might think all this, think me unlearned in the subtleties of the world, but be deceived in thinking so. In fact I know the world, and can distinguish its false subtleties from its true ones.

So to the second quatrain: 'Thus vainely thinking that she thinkes me young', with the usual pun on 'vainely'. Again, the forward movement of the language: a new sentence beginning with 'thus' brings the liars a stage deeper into their mutual deceit, and the sequence of 'thinking...thinkes...although she knowes' stresses with complete and elegant lucidity the confounding of the truth. The structure of this quatrain is different from that of the first: here the first two lines are mounting to a climax, which is reached in the third line: 'Simply I credit her false speaking tongue', after which the movement falls away, but with a clinching weight, in line 8: 'On both sides thus is simple truth supprest'. Two points deserve attention here. Firstly, the play on 'simple'. '*Simply* I credit', that is 'naively'; one remembers the scoff of Autolycus: 'And honesty a very simple gentleman'. But 'simple truth' is the opposite of multiple falsehood: the truth, if only they would tell it, is simpler than all their lying complications. Secondly, the phrase 'her false speaking tongue'. The absence of a hyphen gives us two meanings where its presence would have yielded only one: her false tongue, her speaking (eloquent) tongue. The gain, though small, is real: 'speaking tongue' quietly stresses that though the man knows the woman is lying, he is persuaded nonetheless.

When the sonnet moves (over a colon) from octave to sestet, another stage is entered: the lover's mind is pondering the rationale of the whole business. Two lines of questioning, two lines of answer, in which each partner's attitude is taken in turn. 'O loves best habit is in seeming trust': this is the woman's philosophy, and if this is how she thinks the game is to be played, if this is 'loves best habit', she too, the poem implies, is 'past the best'. In the next line the enfeebled, stroking movement of 'age in *love*, *loves* not

t'have yeares told' hints at the lover's self-dramatization
and self-pity.

The couplet gathers up all that has been suggested in the
previous twelve lines: it is notably crisp and witty, with
the restrained brilliance of its clinching pun: 'Therefore I
lye with her, and she with me', which makes clear the
destination of the whole sonnet, the purpose of the lying;
and clear too (in 'therefore') that no amount of self-
knowledge or of insight into the woman can dissuade the
lover from lying with her in every sense. The line's rhythm
and syntax, 'I lye with her, and she with me', drive home
the mutuality of this state: they shall be two in one flesh,
one in two lies. The last line seems to say that the lovers
who lie with each other (*with* and *to*) are joined together by
two kinds of act and the shared but ambiguous satisfaction
which results. And it may be that there are invisible hyphens
here: 'faults-by-lyes', that is, the acts of love (for want of a
worse word) which the lies procure for them both – though
of course 'by lyes' must also go with 'we flattered be' (and
'flattered', as Seymour-Smith points out, means both 'de-
luded' and 'gratified').

This seems to me one of the most beautifully shaped of
all the Sonnets, a perfect fusion of clear-sightedness and
elegant, poised wit. It is, as Professor Mahood observes,
one of the sonnets 'in which Shakespeare's conflict of feelings is most clearly understood and so most poetically
organised'.[1] And I find her final comment a more satisfying
one than that of Patrick Cruttwell, quoted earlier. She too
quotes him: the final pun, he says, 'forces together the
physical union and its context, as it were, its whole surrounding universe, of moral defilement and falsehood'.[2]
'Yet', as she remarks, 'the total impression of the sonnet is

[1] *Shakespeare's Wordplay*, p. 107. [2] *The Shakespearean Moment*, p. 14.

not one of bitterness, but of acceptance. The lovers need one another in their common weakness. Only a few of the sonnets to the youth show an irony as fully realised and as moving as this.'[1]

Sonnet 129

Such acceptance is rare in the sonnets relating to the mistress. More often the tone is savage, the lover's state of mind deeply, even violently disturbed. This is especially true of the greatest poem in the whole group.

> Th'expence of Spirit in a waste of shame
> Is lust in action, and till action, lust
> Is perjurd, murdrous, blouddy full of blame,
> Savage, extreame, rude, cruell, not to trust,
> Injoyd no sooner but dispised straight,
> Past reason hunted, and no sooner had
> Past reason hated as a swollowed bayt,
> On purpose layd to make the taker mad.
> Mad in pursut[2] and in possession so,
> Had, having, and in quest, to have extreame,
> A blisse in proofe and prov'd a very wo,[3]
> Before a joy proposd behind a dreame,
>   All this the world well knowes yet none knowes well,
>   To shun the heaven that leads men to this hell.

This, obviously, is not directed at the mistress herself. Indeed it is not about the mistress at all, though it rightly belongs among the poems which deal with her: surely it is she, and not the youth, who must be supposed to have provoked such an outburst. But its real subject is the state of lust itself, and its way of handling this makes it a counterpart to the sonnets which express extreme states of exalted

[1] *Shakespeare's Wordplay*, p. 108.
[2] The Quarto reads: 'made In pursut'.
[3] The Quarto reads: 'and very woe'. In the 1967 reprinting of Seymour-Smith's text he has amended this as I have done.

love: poems like 'Let me not to the marriage of true mindes' (116) which so completely transcend the situation from which they spring that we do not even ask, for instance, whether the love expressed is for a woman or a man. Yet neither in those poems nor in 'Th' expence of Spirit' do we feel any remoteness of the speaking voice from the experience it is uttering. How to suggest, in analysis, the twin facts that the propositions about lust all seem to be of general application and yet that the tone is so personal? We instantly recognize how widely the poem ranges: obviously it is not just about one man's predicament, still less a mere moralizing of lust in general, a quiet armchair discussion of the topic. It *is* general, like 'They that have powre', general without being in the least abstract, and yet, in a sense hard to account for, personal as well, the cry of a particular voice. Not idiosyncratic, certainly; *who* the speaker is does not concern us any more than the details of the relationship, which are not supplied. Yet the sense of *a person* focusing the poem's theme is unusually strong. There is a certain resemblance to Donne's 'Hymne to God the Father': both poems are powerfully dramatic, yet neither offers any scene-setting of the usual kind (usual, at least, in Donne). In each the drama is created entirely in the tones and rhythms of the speaking voice. In each, again, the voice is that of a consciousness wrought to an extraordinary intensity.

Is Shakespeare's speaker actually experiencing lust as he speaks? Perhaps not; but the tone suggests that lust is at the one moment understood *and felt* for what it is. The speaker may not be saying, with Ovid, 'I know and approve the better, I follow the worse'; but he does know, intimately, the terrible compulsion towards the 'joy proposd behind a dreame'. This is a 'sin of self-love' in which action is vitiated from the very start by the knowledge that the joy proposed can never be possessed where one persists in hunting it, that the pursuit is 'perjurd' before it begins, and at each step of the way.

Beeching has pointed out that this sonnet, like 66, differs from the rest 'in not being written in quatrains, though the rhymes are so arranged'.[1] The reason for this has already been suggested: to create a sense of urgency the poem develops a powerful momentum of rhythm and syntax, driving over the line-endings and the quatrain-divisions in one long inexorable sentence where word is piled on word and phrase tramples phrase. Throughout, as Robert Graves and Laura Riding have shown,[2] the language re-creates the simultaneous recognition of simultaneous possibilities. It will not do to speak as Hallett Smith does: 'Sonnet 129 is a formal description of lust, with important distinctions among the stages of it: before satisfaction, during satisfaction, and after satisfaction';[3] for as Graves and Riding point out (pp. 119–20), the poem explains

> that lust comprises all the stages of lust: the after-lust period (*Had*) the actual experience of lust (*having*), and the anticipation of lust (*in quest*); and that the extremes of lust are felt in all these stages... Further, one stage in lust is like the others, is as extreme as the others. All the distinctions made in the poem between *lust in action* and *till action lust*, between lust *In pursut* and lust *in possession* are made to show that in the end there are no real distinctions... that lust is all things at all times.

The opening line is rich in suggestions from its key words: 'expence', 'spirit', 'waste', 'of shame', where

[1] Quoted by Rollins, vol. I, p. 174.

[2] See *A Survey of Modernist Poetry* (London, 1927). The passage is reprinted as 'A Study in Original Spelling and Punctuation' in Barbara Herrnstein (ed.), *Discussions of Shakespeare's Sonnets* (Boston, 1964), pp. 116–23. Page references are to the latter.

[3] Hallett Smith, *Elizabethan Poetry* (Cambridge, Mass., 1952), p. 187.

'spirit', for instance, means not only life, vital force, in the still current sense, but also the more technical 'spirit generative',[1] so that the line has a strongly physical, indeed physiological reference, not merely the more generalized, more disembodied meaning we often suppose it to have; where 'waste' picks up one of the senses of 'expense' but suggests 'wilderness' as well; and where 'of shame' means both 'shameful' and 'ashamed'.[2] But in its ensuing development the poem depends hardly at all on this kind of word-play: though the language is closely wrought, its effects are gained by other means.[3] The second and third lines provide an example:

> Is lust in action, and till action, lust
> Is perjurd, murdrous, blouddy full of blame.

In the second half of the line 'lust in action' is turned about, given a new direction, pointed back to the stage *before* action so that that stage too appears as lust and deserves the epithets of line 3 (and line 4) as much as lust in action does. This gives added point to the reversed grammatical order which Hallett Smith notes in the first line and a half: 'Lust in action is the expense of spirit in a waste of shame' (p. 188). But because the expense of spirit can be seen earlier still, it is this which must be named first. An even more important reason is that 'Th' expence of Spirit in a waste of shame' is both an evaluation of lust (which would be submerged if the grammatical order were observed) and the point of the whole poem. But it is lines 2 and 3 that form the bridge, syntactically, between the first line and the

---

[1] As Patrick Cruttwell explains, p. 14.
[2] Graves and Riding, p. 122.
[3] Brian Vickers, in his *Classical Rhetoric in English Poetry* (London, 1970), pp. 160–3, shows how much of the poem's strength comes from its patterning of traditional rhetorical figures.

rest. Once the distinction (which is in fact *no* distinction) has been made between 'in action' and 'before action', we can be launched on the stream of adjectives which lead us, through more simple ('perjurd, murdrous') and then more complex descriptions of the state, into the centre of the whirlpool. Single words give place to short phrases and these in turn to longer phrases and whole lines: 'Injoyd no sooner but dispised straight'; until, with 'Past reason hunted, and no sooner had', the sense and movement drive us beyond the end of one line into the next, the two being linked, in their presentation of *before* and *after*, by the parallel constructions, 'Past reason hunted...past reason hated'. And again, while 'Past reason hated as a swollowed bayt' seems complete and final enough, at the end of breath comes the next line to extend the meaning still further: 'On purpose layd to make the taker mad'.

A textual difficulty follows: should the next line read ' *Made* in pursut' as in the Quarto, or ' *Mad* in pursut' as in modern editions? After the kind of verbal linking I have traced so far, I think both ear and mind are better satisfied by the amended reading: the linking effect '...mad/Mad' is surely important; it is in fact both link and break at once. ('Mad: yes, mad.') The word is carried into the next rush of insight, which it dominates. Rhetorically the repetition is strikingly effective: it seems to have the force of intense passion behind it. 'Made' would seem a weaker effect. But very likely the whole question is one of contemporary pronunciation: if 'mad' and 'made' were sounded alike, an aural play on the two words was most probably intended. (Alternative spellings of 'mad', according to the O.E.D., were 'made' and 'maad'.)

Some further points need making. Firstly, the line 'A blisse in proofe and prov'd a very wo' stresses again what other parts of the poem have implied, that both during and after the act, lust is simultaneously pleasure and pain, 'blisse' and 'wo'. There must be no punctuation or the unity of the idea, of the reality, is destroyed. Secondly, in the next line, the Quarto's lack of punctuation must again be defended:

> Before a joy proposd behind a dreame

conveys more meanings than the one spelt out to the destruction of the rest by modern punctuation:

> Before, a joy proposed; behind, a dream.

Thirdly, in this sonnet the couplet really does clinch all that has been said: the comma before it is justified by more than the momentum built up. And it carries the poem one stage further: 'The force of the second *well* is to deny the first *well*: no one really knows anything of lust except in personal experience, and only through personal experience can lust be known *well* rather than "well-known".' (Graves and Riding, p. 121.) And paradoxically, 'All this' (that is, all that the speaker has just said) is not what 'the world well knowes'; it is much more than that. What the poem offers is not a re-hashing of the commonplaces about lust but a re-creation of what may be learnt of lust by going through it.

Many of the problems in interpreting this sonnet, particularly those that seem to turn on punctuation, are dissolved by reading it aloud. The tongue finds the tone and inflexion of lines as the silent mind cannot. To return to lines 11 and 12:

> A blisse in proofe and prov'd a very wo,
> Before a joy proposd behind a dreame.

Given the speed and pressure already built up in the poem's voice, the lines as the Quarto punctuates them are perfectly right. They contain no punctuation because the voice and the mind of the poem are moving too quickly for that to be an accurate way of indicating the sense: yet different possibilities flash past, and the inflexion of the voice, as it speaks, registers each. Lust is all these things, and the speaker realizes this as he speaks: the speed with which he moves from one word to the next and the next conveys both the rapidity with which the mind perceives the truth and the unity of that truth. The second of the lines can be taken as the modern editors take it; it can also be taken just as it stands: (lust is) facing a joy which lies behind a dream. But only the unpunctuated version realizes the sound and speed of the voice in the context the earlier lines have created, and enables the meaning I have suggested (the chief one, surely) to come through. Certain subtleties of inflexion cannot be caught by any written punctuation at all and may well be obscured or destroyed by it; but the voice, trying the line over, finds them instinctively.

Sonnet 147

The real strength of Sonnet 129 can be seen by putting beside it another sonnet on the same theme and with claims to a similar kind of strength.

> My love is as a feaver longing still,
> For that which longer nurseth the disease,
> Feeding on that which doth preserve the ill,
> Th'uncertaine sicklie appetite to please:
> My reason the Phisition to my love,
> Angry that his prescriptions are not kept
> Hath left me, and I desperate now approve,
> Desire is death, which Phisick did except.
> Past cure I am, now Reason is past care,
> And frantick madde with ever-more unrest,

ιy thoughts and my discourse as mad mens are,
　　At randon from the truth vainely exprest.
　　　For I have sworne thee faire, and thought thee bright,
　　　　Who art as black as hell, as darke as night.

While this is clearly not a weak poem, its strengths are comparatively crude ones. It is in the main well-wrought, but on simple lines. The development of the idea from quatrain to quatrain does give a sense of the lover's steady progress towards the complete inversion of reason and truth, but the verse movement, while never sluggish, is never especially subtle or individual, and the same might be said of the ruling conceit, of love the fever and reason the physician. The main trouble comes in the couplet, which seems over-stated. And as C. L. Barber says (p. 29): ' Where the sonnets to the woman... becomes completely grim, there is usually a certain falsifying simplification in resorting to unmeasured abuse, as in the couplet which ends, but does not resolve, the analysis of love's fever.' The stridency of the couplet, its extremes of black and white, leave us saying not 'Yes' but 'Well, *perhaps*'. If we look back at the closing couplet of 129 we will feel at once how far superior that ending is. Both poems end with 'hell', and the way it is worked into each couplet will show the difference of imaginative quality between the two: 'black as hell' is fairly obvious, 'the heaven that leads men to this hell' has far more internal friction and surprise, and is seen to be justified by all that has gone before it.

*　　　*　　　*

What is needed, it seems, for real power in the confrontation of sins of self-love is evidence in the poetry of a complex awareness, of the capacity to make a complex response to a complex state of affairs. Sonnet 62 shows this to some extent,

138 much more fully, 129 at least as much, though in another way. Beside the second and third of these, 147 must seem in the first twelve lines low-keyed – too close to a poetry of *statement*, even if the statement is made in terms of a conceit – and then at the close of the poem too theatrical.

In the best of these poems the poet genuinely faces the complexities of self-love and they become actual in the poetry; there is an extraordinarily full, extraordinarily honest recognition of fault. The immediacy of the poetry shows us the self indeed.

3

Self-Love and Love Itself

A proper self-love

The Sonnets are concerned with two kinds of self-love; so
far we have seen only the damaging kind. It is time to look
at sonnets which show self-love as a virtue: where the
emphasis shifts from self-love as harmful to self-love as
necessary, if the self is to survive and not to disintegrate.
Shakespeare's sense of the self – his own and that of others –
persists even in the extreme self-renunciation of his love for
the friend. With the mistress, too, despite the disruptive
effect she has on his personality, he never quite loses a
radical awareness of who and what he is.

'When I am worthy of myself', Wordsworth said; and
even at his nadir the poet of the Sonnets strikes us as knowing what his worthier self requires. This needs to be said,
because some readers have found him a passive, even a
supine figure. Yvor Winters puts this view as strongly as
anyone:

In the first place there is in a large number of the poems an attitude
of servile weakness on the part of the poet in the face of the person
addressed; this attitude is commonly so marked as to render a
sympathetic approach to the subject all but impossible, in spite of
any fragmentary brilliance which may be exhibited.[1]

And speaking of Sonnet 66 he says (p. 108): 'Shakespeare

[1] 'Poetic Style in Shakespeare's Sonnets' in Barbara Herrnstein (ed.),
Discussions of Shakespeare's Sonnets, p. 107.

(like Arnold after him, in "Dover Beach") turns aside from the issues he has raised to a kind of despairing sentimentality, and the effect is one of weakness, poetic and personal.' Perhaps surprisingly, the answer to this comes from Bernard Shaw. Of a play about Shakespeare by Frank Harris he says:

Shakespear is presented with the most pathetic tenderness. He is tragic, bitter, pitiable, wretched and broken among a robust crowd of Jonsons and Elizabeths; but to me he is not Shakespear because I miss the Shakespearean irony and the Shakespearean gaiety. Take these away and Shakespear is no longer Shakespear; all the bite, the impetus, the strength, the grim delight in his own power of looking terrible facts in the face with a chuckle, is gone; and you have nothing left but that most depressing of all things: a victim.[1]

That, of course, is just what Winters takes him to be, but then he gives no sign of being able to detect the Shakespearean irony. It is there all the same, and Shaw is right in his account of what it does for Shakespeare's stature. He is right, too, about something else which Winters appears to miss:

the language of the sonnets addressed to [the aristocratic friend], extravagant as it now seems, is *the language of compliment and fashion*, transfigured no doubt by Shakespear's verbal magic, and *hyperbolical...*, but still unmistakeable for anything else than the expression of a friendship delicate enough to be wounded, and a manly loyalty deep enough to be outraged (pp. 765-6).

The words I have italicized remind us of things which cannot be forgotten without at times completely misreading the Sonnets. Often irony and fashionable hyperbole appear together, and in such a way that the first undercuts the second.

[1] George Bernard Shaw, Preface to *The Dark Lady of the Sonnets* in *Prefaces by Bernard Shaw* (London, 1938), pp. 763-4.

But before considering this, we might look at the kind of thing which seems most likely to provoke Winters' attack. We could take the group, Sonnets 33-5:

Full many a glorious morning have I seene,
Flatter the mountaine tops with soveraine eie,
Kissing the golden face the meddowes greene;
Guilding pale streames with heavenly alcumy:
Anon permit the basest cloudes to ride,
With ougly rack on his celestiall face,
And from the for-lorne world his visage hide
Stealing unseene to west with this disgrace:
Even so my Sunne one early morne did shine,
With all triumphant splendor on my brow,
But out alack, he was but one houre mine,
The region cloude hath mask'd him from me now.
    Yet him for this, my love no whit disdaineth,
    Suns of the world may staine, where heavens sun staineth.

Why didst thou promise such a beautious day,
And make me travaile forth without my cloake,
To let bace cloudes ore-take me in my way,
Hiding thy brav'ry in their rotten smoke.
Tis not enough that through the cloude thou breake,
To dry the raine on my storme-beaten face,
For no man well of such a salve can speake,
That heales the wound, and cures not the disgrace:
Nor can thy shame give phisicke to my griefe,
Though thou repent, yet I have still the losse,
Th'offenders sorrow lends but weake reliefe
To him that beares the strong offenses losse.
    Ah but those teares are pearle which thy love sheeds,
    And they are ritch, and ransome all ill deeds.

No more bee greev'd at that which thou hast done,
Roses have thornes, and silver fountaines mud,
Cloudes and eclipses staine both Moone and Sunne,
And loathsome canker lives in sweetest bud.
All men make faults, and even I in this,

66

Authorizing thy trespas with compare,
My selfe corrupting salving thy amisse,
Excusing thy sins more then thy sins are:
For to thy sensuall fault I bring in sence,
Thy adverse party is thy Advocate,
And gainst my selfe a lawfull plea commence,
Such civill war is in my love and hate,
 That I an accessary needs must be,
 To that sweet theefe which sourely robs from me.

The first thing to notice is the progression of moods and attitudes through these three sonnets. The first consists largely of 'hyperbolical' praise of the friend ('my Sunne') followed by a profession of the poet's lowliness:

> But out alack, he was but one houre mine,
> The region cloude hath mask'd him from me now.

Yet even here the image is not quite so hyperbolical as it may seem: the sun '*permit*[s] the basest cloudes' to obscure it, and so, it seems, does that other sun, the friend. And while 'disgrace' is applied to the actual sun, the word's implications tend to rub off on the metaphorical one: a word for the wise, perhaps. So far, no reproof; and the couplet recognizes, and seems to accept, that what happens in the heavens can also happen here: 'Suns of the world may staine, where heavens sun staineth.'

In the next sonnet, while the early imagery is the same, from the very first words the tone is quite different: intimate, simple, reproachful. A lesser poet, a lesser man, might have pretended not to be hurt or angry, especially if he were a sycophant of the person addressed. But hurt and anger, being part of the experience, must be given expression: it is controlled, certainly, it is not an outburst, but it might well be something even harder for the friend to bear.

> Why didst thou promise such a beautious day...?
> Tis not enough that through the cloude thou breake.

67

The control, besides giving weight and edge to the reproof, conveys the impression that whatever the friend has done, he should have realized what effect it would have on the poet. This sonnet is dramatic in a way that few of Shakespeare's are: it implies a scene, even a 'scene', with successive stages of expostulation and reply, the poet's demands on the youth's shame and loyalty growing increasingly harder to bear with equanimity, until, with the final couplet, the response is tears, and the poet half-regrets, perhaps, the pressure he has put on the youth, and so moves quickly and generously to forgiveness. 'Ah but those teares are pearle which thy love sheeds'. This impulse carries over into the next sonnet, in the desire to allay the friend's distress: 'No more bee greev'd at that which thou has done'. Yet this very generosity, as he sees almost at once, compromises him:

> All men make faults, and even I in this,
> Authorizing thy trespas with compare,
> My selfe corrupting salving thy amisse,
> Excusing thy sins more then thy sins are.

Beyond anything encountered so far, the central insight of this poem is a moral one: if you attempt to excuse the sin of those you love, you may yourself be guilty of sin; in taking their sin upon you, you take with it some of its corruption. And this insight is inseparable from others: that although selves may become involved with each other they remain separate identities separately answerable for their destinies, and that it may even be worse for a man to find excuse for a friend's fault than it was for the friend to commit it. The first fault is merely 'sensual' (performed at the bidding of the senses), the second a matter of 'sense' (that is, reason): a distinction resembling the traditional one between sins of the flesh and sins of the spirit. The imagery, as often in the

Sonnets, could carry more than one set of implications: 'Roses have thornes, and silver fountaines mud'. The fault is thus 'authorized with compare' to the natural defects of purely sensory things, and so (despite the bluntness of that final word 'mud') it is made to seem less reprehensible. Yet the friend is not a rose or a fountain, he is a human and therefore a moral being, and this fact, lurking beneath the images, undermines their argument. Such 'compare', however much the poet would like it to be valid, is a falsification, as he recognizes.

These are not poems of 'servile weakness on the part of the poet'. To take the most doubtful case first: the third sonnet may be anything but muscular and aggressive but the poet here faces and forces into words a painful truth. This in itself is, as I said of Sonnet 94, a sign of moral strength. As for the two earlier sonnets: in the first the oblique firmness of the imagery leaves the friend in no doubt that he is under judgment, and in the second the tone of wounded love carries its own strong authority: 'Tis not enough... / Though thou repent, yet I have still the shame': the voice speaks with unanswerable justice.

If the poet's attitude seems at times a weak one, reflection will often show that it is nothing of the kind. Often he is simply telling the truth, though the truth may not be as simple as it appears. To give an obvious example, 'Farewell thou art too deare for my possessing'[1] may at first seem a beautifully sad and noble gesture of renunciation, but the next line, 'And like enough thou knowst thy *estimate*', will send the mind back to revalue 'possessing' and, still more carefully, 'deare'. The play of attitudes throughout this poem is subtle and delicate, the imagery suggesting that in

[1] Sonnet 87. A precise and admirable account of it is to be found in M.M. Mahood, *Shakespeare's Wordplay*, pp. 108-9.

the youth's sense of his value, there may be both calculation and justice, so that the poet, with a humility which seems realistic rather than servile, renounces his claims upon him. It is not weakness but a heart-rending honesty which sounds in the couplet:

> Thus have I had thee as a dreame doth flatter,
> In sleepe a King, but waking no such matter.

What we encounter, then, is an unusual mingling of irony with acknowledgement of limitations. These two features recur, singly or together, in sonnet after sonnet, and even where the irony is missing or played down, the complete openness, which in another man might well arouse our embarrassment, even our contempt, remains extraordinarily dignified. I am not sure how this can be explained. Perhaps the honesty itself is extraordinary both in kind and degree. There are no half-truths in it, no self-deceptions passing unrecognized; and it is the admixture of these which makes the lip curl when so many hearts are apparently laid bare. Half-truths and self-pity: and as a rule the Sonnets so fully comprehend this, when it is present, that the remaining objection drops away.

Of course, in discussing Sonnet 87, I may have underestimated the irony. In the Sonnets, its extent, as I have tried to show earlier, is often hard to gauge. Here, for instance, one cannot be sure whether the low estimate of the poet is his own or the youth's; whether, indeed, the whole account of their respective merits is not the youth's. (And the youth has the upper hand: 'For how do I hold thee but by thy granting?') To the poet, since he is sadly resigned to the situation and is withdrawing, it hardly matters whether the estimate of things is the friend's or that of others. It is clear that some irony is present, and along with it a completely dignified if bitter resignation.

In Sonnet 57, the irony is of such a kind that some readers miss it altogether: readers, especially, of Professor Winters' kind, who if they find a plain meaning will not look for another.

> Being your slave what should I doe but tend,
> Upon the houres, and times of your desire?
> I have no precious time at al to spend;
> Nor services to doe til you require.
> Nor dare I chide the world without end houre,
> Whilst I (my soveraine) watch the clock for you,
> Nor thinke the bitternesse of absence sowre,
> When you have bid your servant once adieue.
> Nor dare I question with my jealious thought,
> Where you may be, or your affaires suppose,
> But like a sad slave stay and thinke of nought
> Save where you are, how happy you make those.
>   So true a foole is love, that in your Will,
>   (Though you doe any thing) he thinkes no ill.

Here once more is the fashionable extravagance and hyperbole, the courtly and Petrarchan language of lowly devotion to the beloved. But isn't it, while very beautiful, just a little overdone? The movement of the first two lines, for example, is not merely graceful, it is mannered: perhaps the vassalage is being laid on a trifle heavily? And what precisely is the tone of 'I have no precious time at al to spend'? Or rather, the tones. For it seems to me that this line, and indeed the whole poem, can be read in one tone and then again in another. We can read it 'straight' and it will seem beautiful but a trifle fulsome. Or we can take the exaggerations as indicating irony: the rise of the voice in the third line, the greater swell required by the fifth ('Nor dare I chide the world without end houre'), the ritual phrases which are yet, one feels, deliberately too-conspicuous: 'my soveraine', 'your servant', 'like a sad slave'. Taking its bearings from these, the reading will make of the poem a sustained and subtly devastating protest against the treatment the poet has had to endure. Miss Mahood's comment on the end of the next sonnet could hardly be bettered for this one: what we hear, she says, 'may be the voice of a man prostrate with adoration or of one querulous with impatience – "You think this is what I am made for, do you?"'.[1] This catches the ambivalence exactly. But in suggesting this interpretation, we need not go to excess like Seymour-Smith (p. 141): a tone of 'heavily sarcastic bitterness', he comments, with no suggestion of anything else. And again, of lines 3 and 4: 'Forthright and even savage irony, reflected in the rhythm, rescues Shakespeare's state of subservience from utter pusillanimity'; lines 5 to 8 'establish without doubt the bitterly sarcastic tone'. Here is a reader at the opposite extreme from the one who finds no irony at all. Both are wrong; Seymour-Smith because he grossly magnifies the poem's quiet delicate voice and because he seems deaf to any other. But in fact there are two voices which can be heard speaking simultaneously. The friend is meant, I think, to take the poem first as an effusive and oh-so-sad compliment, and only later to do the double-take: 'Did he really mean that? I don't suppose he was being sarcastic?' Precisely because the sonnet is equivocal its protest is the more effective. But of course, the protest is largely qualified by the fact that what the poet says is quite literally true: he does hang about, watching the clock, waiting for the friend to come. Love *has* made him 'a sad slave', 'so true a foole'. There is in the poetry a kind of verbal shrugging of the shoulders and a rueful half-smile, especially in the couplet. It is the fact that the poet sees himself in

[1] *Shakespeare's Wordplay*, p. 109.

these two ways at once that makes it possible and even essential to hear the two tones together throughout the poem.

There is, of course, real point in Seymour-Smith's remark about the saving irony. If the irony were not there, Shakespeare would indeed cut a pathetic figure. The irony is a great deal more than protest: it is not just a way of hitting back at the friend for humiliating him. It is at the same time a mode of self-knowledge and a kind of self-assertion: he can see himself from an extra point of view and can thus, to some extent, transcend his predicament. Since the irony operates against the friend as well as himself, each of them is seen with some measure of liberating detachment. The poet may be the youth's sad slave, which reflects no credit on the slave, but the friend's imperfections are seen as well: he may call forth a love 'this side idolatry' but he can behave badly just the same, and his lover can say so.

He does, again and again: not only in this sonnet but in others already discussed, and in many more. This brings me back to Shaw's stimulating and perceptive comments, and to the charges of weakness, pusillanimity, sycophancy.

A sycophant does not tell his patron that his fame will survive, not in the renown of his own actions, but in the sonnets of his sycophant. A sycophant, when his patron cuts him out in a love affair, does not tell his patron exactly what he thinks of him. Above all, a sycophant does not write to his patron precisely as he feels on all occasions; and this rare kind of sincerity is all over the sonnets. Shakespear, we are told, was 'a very civil gentleman'. This must mean that his desire to please people and be liked by them, and his reluctance to hurt their feelings, led him into amiable flattery even when his feelings were not strongly stirred. If this be taken into account...we shall see more civility and hyperbole than sycophancy even in the earlier and more coldblooded sonnets.[1]

[1] Preface to *The Dark Lady of the Sonnets*, p. 766.

If this, which seems to me apt, is taken together with the claim that Shakespeare is *not* 'that most depressing of all things: a victim', it constitutes a strong defence of the poet: he is neither victim of the Dark Lady nor sycophant of the Fair Friend. And in the poems examined so far it is abundantly clear that irony and a certain noble honesty are the chief marks of his freedom and independence. There is little that can be done to a man with these qualities, no matter how generous and therefore vulnerable his heart is. If a man sets himself at nought, as Shakespeare so frequently does, and yet so manifestly and fully exists, he has triumphed over his circumstances: he is to be seen 'as having nothing and possessing all things'.

Lastly, something might be said about those sonnets[1] in which the poet acknowledges a more than physical absence from the friend – 'That I have frequent binne with unknown mindes' (117) – and yet ends (in 121 and 124 especially) by affirming a great deal besides guilt. For these are again poems of self-knowledge, and more, of self-acceptance: if the poet begins in contrition he ends in charity towards himself; which may sound more comfortable than it is. These sonnets are the counterpart of the three with which this chapter begins. Now it is the poet who has offended and the friend who must forgive. The beautifully cadenced protestations of 109 (which opens the sequence) raise the main issues, yet may be felt to take them a little too easily:

> O never say that I was false of heart,
> Though absence seem'd my flame to quallifie,
> As easie might I from my selfe depart,
> As from my soule which in thy brest doth lye:
> That is my home of love, if I have rang'd,

---

[1] Sonnets 109–12, 117–21, 123–4. The first two of these sets are well discussed by C. L. Barber, pp. 29–30.

Like him that travels I returne againe,
. . .
Never beleeve though in my nature raign'd,
All frailties that besiege all kindes of blood,
That it could so preposterouslie be stain'd,
To leave for nothing all thy summe of good:

'Water' is needed for the poet's 'staine', but this he himself can provide. One is to suppose, I think, that the self-examination has not gone very deep so far. In the next two sonnets, more painful admissions are made:

Alas 'tis true, I have gone here and there,
And made my selfe a motley to the view,
Gor'd mine own thoughts, sold cheap what is most deare.

'Gor'd mine own thoughts' means much more, of course, than Seymour-Smith's anaemic gloss, 'been untrue to my deepest beliefs', which gets none of the physical associations of stabbing, piercing, covering with blood. This, more gravely confronted now, is what it means to be governed by 'all frailties that besiege all kindes of blood'. And yet sin is behovely:

by all above,
These blenches gave my heart an other youth,
And worse essaies prov'd thee my best of love,
Now all is done, have what shall have no end.

Even here, then, blessings flow from the fall, and in the next sonnet's image of a 'nature. . . subdu'd/To what it workes in, like the Dyers hand' we and the friend are prompted to a sense of inevitability. The poet is admitting his fault, asking pardon for it ('Pitty me then, and wish I were renu'de'), but also acknowledging his nature, which is not the same thing at all. If, in the words of Sonnet 117, he has 'hoysted saile to al the windes', then not only does he 'returne rebukt to [his] content' (119), but his final word on the

episode, spoken in 121, is an acceptance of himself with all
his faults and a dismissal of what the world may say of him,
true or false.

> Tis better to be vile then vile esteemed,
> When not to be, receives reproach of being.

Immediately this seems to imply that others have spoken
falsely of him, but while this may be the occasion of the
reflections here, the effect of the poem is to set the self, with
all its imperfections, against its calumniators:

> Noe, I am that I am, and they that levell
> At my abuses, reckon up their owne.

Here, says Wilson Knight, Shakespeare 'asserts a kind of
beyond-good-and-evil claim for himself'.[1] Not quite; but
the poem, in its context, certainly reads like a self-affirma-
tion, and a balanced one at that: there is no note of apology,
no 'servile weakness' before either the friend or the world.
This, like the better-known Sonnet 146 ('Poore soule the
center of my sinfull earth') is the 'song of a man who has
come through'. And Sonnet 124 is the song of a love that
has come through.

> Yf my deare love were but the childe of state,
> It might for fortunes basterd be unfathered,
> As subject to times love, or to times hate,
> Weeds among weeds, or flowers with flowers gatherd.
> No it was buylded far from accident,
> It suffers not in smilinge pomp, nor falls
> Under the blow of thralled discontent,
> Whereto th'inviting time our fashion calls:
> It fears not policy that *Hericke*,
> Which workes on leases of short numbred howers,
> But all alone stands hugely pollitick,
> That it nor growes with heat, nor drownes with showres.

[1] G. Wilson Knight, *The Mutual Flame* (London, 1955), p. 14.

To this I witnes call the foles of time,
Which die for goodnes, who have liv'd for crime.

Such poems consolidate the spiritual gains won from the
vicissitudes with which the sequence deals. The poet's self
and the poet's love have resisted attack from within and
from without. They stand out 'hugely pollitick', like
towers above surrounding ruins. It is in the context of
vicissitude and flux that 124[1] asks us to see the 'deare love'
which it celebrates. *Which*, not *whom*: for of course, it is not
the youth who is spoken of here, but the poet's love.[2] If this
is centred in the youth it is something far more than a love
for a single individual. That individual may have begotten
the love in the first place, and may be its embodiment, but
what he embodies is an absolute, as the language of the
sonnet makes plain. The reality proclaimed here transcends
the individual person, poet and beloved, in whom it is
realized; it transcends, too, the forces of 'mutability',
whether they be at work in the individual life, in the larger
affairs of man ('state', 'policy'), or in the whole universe of
accident and time, with its love and hate, its weeds and
flowers.

Love

This prompts a fuller consideration of what 'love' may
mean in the Sonnets. It means, indeed, a range of things,
and we cannot be concerned only with the transcendent
moments of sonnets like the one just mentioned. To emphasize this, we might approach the subject from an unexpected
direction:

[1] See Arthur Mizener's detailed analysis of this poem: 'The Structure of
Figurative Language in Shakespeare's Sonnets' in Barbara Herrnstein
(ed.), *Discussions of Shakespeare's Sonnets*, pp. 137–51.
[2] M. M. Mahood, 'Love's Confin'd Doom', p. 60.

> My Mistres eyes are nothing like the Sunne,
> Currall is farre more red, then her lips red,
> If snow be white, why then her brests are dun:
> If haires be wiers, black wiers grow on her head:
> I have seene Roses damaskt, red and white,
> But no such Roses see I in her cheekes,
> And in some perfumes is there more delight,
> Then in the breath that from my Mistres reekes.
> I love to heare her speake, yet well I know,
> That Musicke hath a farre more pleasing sound:
> I graunt I never saw a goddesse goe,
> My Mistres when shee walkes treads on the ground.
>   And yet by heaven I thinke my love as rare,
>   As any she beli'd with false compare.

(Sonnet 130)

This is deservedly well known as a piece of literary satire, and is sometimes dismissed as nothing more. That is a mistake: for all its lightness it is a serious poem, and it does more than satirize a way of writing, though it does that very well. While there is no point in pretending that it is among the most heavily-freighted of the Sonnets, and while the satirical element is prominent, the poem, like most good satire, has something to affirm. The humour, of course, is not altogether at the expense of bad love poetry:

> If snow be white, why then her brests are dun...
> My Mistres when shee walkes treads on the ground.

But it is wrong to picture her, as Sir John Gielgud does when he recites this on stage, as tramping through life on broad and heavy feet: the poetry is subtler than that. Without resorting to low comedy, Shakespeare is simply saying that his mistress is no goddess but a mortal woman; the contrast, essentially, is between the conventional poetic mistress and this real one. The real one, it is true, hardly reaches an acceptable level of beauty: dun breasts (to go no further) would seem rather less than that. But perhaps the poet's humour darkens them a little to suggest that by comparison with the snowy complexions of Petrarchan loves, any actual woman's skin must appear to disadvantage. Yet even the playing-down of her beauty suggests a feeling for the woman's own particular attributes.

Here, as in so many of the sonnets to the friend, we see Shakespeare's preference for the unique, the actual, as opposed to idealized abstractions. His mistress's eyes are nothing like the sun, her cheeks lack the prescribed roses, her voice is not as musical as it might be, *and yet*... The couplet has real point: it clinches the poem beautifully and extends its range. For the poet is both attacking conventional beauty and paying his mistress a real compliment, that of recognizing her as a real woman, whom he finds compelling in spite of the fact that her qualities are if anything the opposite of the accepted ones. Or rather, *because* of that. 'She is an individual, and her style of attractiveness is individual.'[1] Her truth is better than any of the usual lies: she gives the lie to the grossly exaggerated praise lavished (poetically) on others. The couplet, indeed the whole poem, states lightly but not (in the end) flippantly an attitude we find throughout the Sonnets, and for that matter, throughout the plays: the rejection of falsity, whether of heart, of speech or of appearance (to look no further than Sonnet 67: 'Why should false painting immitate his cheeke?' or 68: 'Before these bastard signes of faire were borne'), and the praise of whatever is plain, honest, direct, natural, genuine. For Shakespeare as for Donne, lovers are themselves when 'true plaine hearts do in the faces rest'. Love is based on a recognition of 'the other', and of the uniqueness of the other; and whatever else Shakespeare may say of the mis-

[1] Patrick Cruttwell, *The Shakespearean Moment*, p. 36.

tress in later sonnets, she is always seen as herself. While there is something deeply destructive about this relationship it is not that the poet deceives himself into seeing her as the embodiment of desirable beauty. On the contrary: he knows she is not that, and does not want her to be; but knowing what she is he still pursues her. The whole relationship, with this poem as a sort of scherzo on the dominant motif, might be seen as demonstrating in one set of terms what love-relationships are really like. But this is matter for another chapter. What needs to be emphasized now is that even here we find Shakespeare's characteristic awareness of the other person as someone unstereotyped, unpredictable, unique.

Having raised this point because it should be kept constantly in mind, I now want to discuss the two relationships with which the sequence is concerned. The easiest starting-point is the one Shakespeare himself provides.

> Two loves I have of comfort and dispaire,
> Which like two spirits do sugiest me still,
> The better angell is a man right faire:
> The worser spirit a woman collour'd il.
> To win me soone to hell my femall evill,
> Tempteth my better angel from my side,
> And would corrupt my saint to be a divel:
> Wooing his purity with her fowle pride.
> And whether that my angel be turn'd finde,
> Suspect I may, yet not directly tell,
> But being both from me both to each friend,
> I gesse one angel in an others hel.
> > Yet this shal I nere know but live in doubt,
> > Till my bad angel fire my good one out.
>
> (Sonnet 144)

While Sonnet 1 introduces the major themes, here we are given a statement of the central situations; and more, for

these are shown, on the level of plot, to be linked, so that
the two loves, however opposed they may be, appear as the
two aspects of a single experience, a single pattern.

Before we come to this sonnet we already know (on the
Quarto's arrangement) most of what it tells us, but the
evidence is scattered. It is clear that the love for the youth
is, on the whole, one of comfort: many sonnets have shown
the nature of this comfort and some of them will shortly be
examined. It is equally clear why the apparently more
'normal' relationship is one of despair: even if we set aside
Sonnet 129, most of the sonnets so far addressed to the
mistress testify to the troubled passion she inspires. It is
hinted at in the couplet of 131: 'In nothing art thou blacke
save in thy deeds', and more than hinted at in 137: 'Thou
blinde foole love, what doost thou to mine eyes?' 'Corrupt
by over-partiall lookes', they are 'anchord in the baye
where all men ride'. It is clear, too, that not only the poet,
but the youth as well, has become involved with the mistress: Sonnets 40–2 appear to refer to this; Sonnet 133 undoubtedly does:

> Beshrew that heart that makes my heart to groane
> For that deepe wound it gives my friend and me;
> I'st not ynough to torture me alone,
> But slave to slavery my sweet'st friend must be.
> Me from my selfe thy cruell eye hath taken,
> And my next selfe thou harder hast ingrossed,
> Of him, my selfe, and thee I am forsaken,
> A torment thrice three-fold thus to be crossed:

And now 144 recapitulates, emphasizing the pattern: youth
and mistress, angel and devil, both 'suggest' the poet, each
according to his own nature, his own colour, as it were, and
the 'female evil' tempts the youth as well. If she succeeds,

both friend and poet (since the friend is the poet's other and better self) will soon be won to 'hell'; and that, as line 12 makes plain enough, means more than one thing here.

What is the significance of this situation? We must look, on the one hand, to the love conventions of Shakespeare's time; on the other, to the spiritual realities with which the Sonnets are concerned and which the 'two loves', and their suspected entanglement, reveal.

In the other love poetry of the time the dominant convention is of course the Petrarchan, and its features are well known. I am chiefly concerned with the central situation: the poet's love for a 'cruel fair'. Originally, before her attitude becomes trivialized into mere perversity or coyness, the cruelty is necessary: bound to another and also virtuous, she *must* deny herself to the poet. In sixteenth-century English poetry this significance survives, albeit among a good deal of debased matter. The survival is not surprising since the realities to which the Petrarchan convention points are abiding human ones: above all else, the longing for the unattainable, which the convention localizes in terms of the lover's passion for a mistress beyond his reach. And at the heart of this there is a 'moral component', as C.P. Snow would say of science and as Denis de Rougement has shown in his far-reaching study of the Tristan myth.[1] The Petrarchan convention not only gives expression to the lover's unfulfilled yearnings for his mistress: it represents (if Rougement is right) the sublimation of desires conceived as forbidden. Hence, for example, through the mechanism of the mistress who returns the poet's love but is faithful to her marriage vows, we get the conflict between desire and honour expressed in one of the songs in *Astrophel and Stella*:

[1] Denis de Rougemont, *Passion and Society* (London, 1960).

There his hands in their speech, faine
Would have made tongue's language plaine;
But her hands his hands repelling,
Gave repulse all grace excelling.

Then she spake; her speech was such,
As not eares but hart did tuch:
While such wise she love denied,
As yet love she signified...

'Trust me while I thee deny,
In my selfe the smart I try,
Tyran honour doth thus use thee,
Stella's selfe might not refuse thee.

'Therefore, Deere, this no more move,
Least, though I leave not thy love,
Which too deep in me is framed,
I should blush when thou art named.'[1]

How much of the Petrarchan convention do Shakespeare's
Sonnets accept? At first glance, very little, but it would be
wrong to think that Shakespeare simply abandons it; wrong
also to say, as I have heard said, that perhaps he didn't
really know what the convention was: the early comedies
show conclusively that he did. But he took from it what
seemed to him valuable, affirming in his own terms those
truths of human experience which the Petrarchan convention came into existence, and stayed in existence, to express.
In the Sonnets he seems heedless of it for much of the time
(Sonnet 130 is the most notable exception), but by his own
route he arrives at the same destination as those poets who
really *used* the convention: who found in it and gave to it a
human significance, and didn't merely gabble off a formula
learned by rote and drained of any meaning it might have

---

[1] *Astrophel and Stella* (Eighth song), in *The Poems of Sir Philip Sidney*, ed.
William A. Ringler, Jr (Oxford, 1962), pp. 219–20.

had. Perhaps without being fully aware of what he was doing, he gave to the convention a startlingly new form. It seems unlikely that the Sonnets were deliberately conceived either as a parallel or as a critique of Petrarchan love, yet in effect they are both. Leslie Fiedler is right enough in saying: 'in the end one reads the complete sequence not as the mere confession of an erotic misadventure but as a study of love itself as understood in Western Europe towards the end of the sixteenth century.'[1]

In Shakespeare's sequence it is important that the mistress should not be the conventional one. Her role is different; the conventional role is transferred to another player. The first group of sonnets (1–126) offers not a woman but a youth as 'beauty's pattern', the living embodiment of the lover's noblest aspirations. (That he falls short in some ways doesn't alter this.) In all essentials it is he who is the Petrarchan mistress ('the Master Mistris of my passion'): he is beautiful, he prompts the lover's highest idealism, and he is inaccessible. That is, as with the Petrarchan mistress, the love can have no sexual consummation: the principle in each case is the same. The Petrarchan lover, clearly enough, experiences sexual desire, even if its physical expression is out of the question. With Shakespeare one senses its presence too, and for temperamental as well as moral reasons its consummation is again out of the question. If possible, more so: the poet's love for the youth, while it is homosexual in character, is not so in action; Sonnet 20 shows us that. When we turn from the quasi-Petrarchan youth to an anti-Petrarchan mistress, there are no grounds for idealism at all. It is one of the functions of Sonnet 130 to make that utterly

---

[1] Leslie A. Fiedler, 'Some Contexts of Shakespeare's Sonnets' in Edward Hubler (ed.), *The Riddle of Shakespeare's Sonnets* (New York, 1962), p. 82. I am indebted to this article for some ideas incorporated in the early part of this chapter.

plain: this is no conventional beloved, and neither the lover's emotions nor the whole relationship will be of the expected kind.

> Therefore I lye with her, and she with me,
> And in our faults by lyes we flattered be.   (138)

> For I have sworne thee faire, and thought thee bright,
> Who art as black as hell, as darke as night.   (147)

> No want of conscience hold it that I call,
> Her love, for whose deare love I rise and fall.   (151)

The dark woman indeed is everything the Petrarchan mistress is not, except in one particular: her capacity to obsess the poet's imagination. And then, obviously, with very different consequences.

There remains the other, the spiritual, significance of the situation in the Sonnets, particularly as it is revealed by 144. At some points it has been touched on already. Much of what still needs to be said is dealt with in *The Mutual Flame* by Wilson Knight (pp. 23ff.). Of Shakespeare's love for the youth he says: 'We must not deny a strong sexual impulse'; and yet, though like Marvell's parallel lines in 'The Definition of Love' they never meet, 'the love, at its best moments, does not seem tragic; indeed, we somehow feel it the grander and more perfect in that physical intercourse goes no farther than "eyes"... That is not to say that the poetry is unphysical, or spiritual in any limited and doctrinal sense' (p. 25). Wilson Knight goes on to juxtapose the 'homosexual idealism' of the love for the youth against the 'heterosexual passion, or lust' for the mistress, and then to suggest that this antithesis is that of Nietzsche's Apollonian and Dionysian principles: the youth being Apollonian, the mistress Dionysian. The two are brought together in Sonnet 144 and in the situation it speaks of: 'Whether or not it ever happened, it is right that the lady should be suspected of having seduced the youth', for in this relationship we are made aware of 'the intertwining of good and evil, and it would be an error to regard the evil as, in the last resort, an intruder. They are necessarily involved in each other, and somehow both must be assimilated' (p. 29). This, it becomes clear, is not a pattern of abstract ideas for Shakespeare; it is a matter of temperament. Shakespeare is capable of 'physical and sexual attraction' towards the Apollonian youth and of lust for the Dionysian mistress, because his own nature is a dual one. To Wyndham Lewis, quoted by Wilson Knight (p. 30), Shakespeare is a 'sort of feminine genius' and his general attitude is 'that of a woman'. Hence a recurrent disgust (in the plays as well as the Sonnets) with hetero-sexual experience; hence, too, the fact that (in Knight's words now) 'It is always his women, rather than his men, whose love-poetry is most convincing: . . . they are his voices, and. . . may be said to represent the feminine aspects of [his] own self, or soul' (p. 31). All this leads to the conclusion that

The creative consciousness is bisexual; otherwise there could be no creation; and in representing the poet's engagements with both sexes, the Sonnets describe steps on the path towards the creative integration. . . The total content is not confined to love and lust: we are shown these in relation to each other, and to poetry, true and false. . . (p. 33).

And further:

The integration must indeed use the whole complex state, good and evil, all of it; but nevertheless we can point to certain high moments of positive experience that appear to be the ideal striven for. Such are found in the poet's love for the youth. And yet this ideal, to be an ideal, must itself somehow contain the whole; must have at least

86

something of the Dionysian as well as the Apollonian; and it has, in various ways (p. 34).

One sign of this is the element of desire in the poet's love; another is the youth's involvement with the mistress (and apparently with others as well); then too, while there are 'moments of unity when the poet feels at one with his friend', the friend 'possesses also a peculiar unity; and Shakespeare is bound for another unity' (p. 35).

I have quoted from Wilson Knight at such length because I know of no critic who is so penetrating on this subject. At times the balance is precarious and the path crazy, but he arrives at his destination: he makes sense of the love in the Sonnets, and his account is needed if we are to understand the nature of Shakespearean love and see how at a deep level its various manifestations cohere. The two loves are profoundly related in Shakespeare's multiple personality: that personality of which he himself is aware in Sonnet 121:

> Noe, I am that I am, and they that levell
> At my abuses, reckon up their owne,
> I may be straight though they them-selves be bevel;
> By their rancke thoughts, my deedes must not be shown.

Critics have laid much stress on the nobility and generosity of the Sonnets, on the extraordinary degree of self-abnegation in the love they express. Thus C. L. Barber:

Many of the sonnets are wonderfully generous poems; they *give* meaning and beauty. The generosity is at once personal, a selfless love, and impersonal, the glow upon the world at the golden moment when Shakespeare began to write. The poems create a world resonant with the friend's beauty.[1]

And C. S. Lewis:

The self-abnegation, the 'naughting', in the *Sonnets* never rings

[1] 'An Essay on the Sonnets', p. 11.

false. This patience, this anxiety (more like a parent's than a lover's) to find excuses for the beloved, this clear-sighted and wholly unembittered resignation, this transference of the whole self into another self without the demand for a return, have hardly a precedent in profane literature.[1]

True enough; yet neither of these passages quite suggests the peculiar strength of this love. It is easy to be noble and generous if one is blind to some of the facts. As earlier discussion (especially of 94, 33–5, 57) has shown, it would be a mistake to see this love as one of perfect harmony and acceptance, unshadowed by any trouble in events and untinged with irony in the poet's awareness. This view would miss much of the spiritual triumph which the Sonnets record. Enough, however, has been said about Shakespeare's irony, whether directed at himself, at the friend or at the mistress. It is time to look at poems where the overriding note is one of selfless praise: poems which in effect say simply, 'You are you',[2] or poems which are impersonal in the sense that the 'you' and the 'I' are both dissolved in the contemplation of love itself. I should like to consider three sonnets known to every reader of English poetry. In the first place, Sonnet 116:

> Let me not to the marriage of true mindes
> Admit impediments, love is not love
> Which alters when it alteration findes,
> Or bends with the remover to remove.
> O no, it is an ever fixed marke
> That lookes on tempests and is never shaken;
> It is the star to every wandring barke,
> Whose worths unknowne, although his higth be taken.
> Lov's not Times foole, though rosie lips and cheeks
> Within his bending sickles compasse come,

---

[1] *English Literature in the Sixteenth Century*, p. 505.
[2] 'Who is it that sayes most, which can say more,
    Then this rich praise, that you alone, are you' (Sonnet 84).

Love alters not with his breefe houres and weekes,
But beares it out even to the edge of doome:
  If this be error and upon me proved,
  I never writ, nor no man ever loved.

One great difficulty in discussing this sonnet is that for most of us it is too well-known. Like Gray's *Elegy* it has become a part of us, and, as Johnson said of Gray's poem, it 'abounds with images which find a mirror in every mind, and with sentiments to which every bosom returns an echo.'[1] While it is 'original' (as Johnson went on to say of part of the *Elegy*) in the sense that only Shakespeare could have written it, it is much like the *Elegy* in being the very opposite of a personal statement in the limited sense: he who reads these sentiments persuades himself that he has always felt them. Shakespeare the individual, even perhaps Shakespeare the individual poet, is seen here, as in many others of the greatest sonnets, to be subsumed into a larger humanity. As J.B. Leishman says, this is 'an utterance in which even the greatest of poets seems to have become completely merged into something greater, and in which we seem to hear, no longer merely the poet, but love itself defying Time'.[2] The simplicity of the vocabulary, I think, has a lot to do with this: 'the poet', as Tucker Brooke observed, 'has employed one hundred and ten of the simplest words in the language, and the two simplest rime-schemes, to produce a poem which has about it no strangeness whatever except the strangeness of perfection.'[3] And the strangeness of the poem's perfection is only exceeded by the strangeness of talking about it at all; but at least it can do no harm.

[1] Samuel Johnson, 'Thomas Gray', in *Lives of the English Poets* (London, 1925), vol. II, p. 392.
[2] *Themes and Variations in Shakespeare's Sonnets*, p. 56.
[3] Quoted in Rollins, vol. I, p. 294.

Despite what has been said about its impersonality, despite the strong sense of 'love itself defying Time', the sonnet is in one way remarkably personal. Remembering its great statements ('love is...love is not'), we tend to forget how important are the words 'I' and 'me' in the first and last lines: they are assimilated quickly into our response to the statements they enfold. Yet those statements, indeed the poem as a whole, would strike us differently if they were not there. The voice is that of one man, speaking with the resonance of profound conviction.

'The marriage of true mindes'. Here as elsewhere in the poem we find that the simplicity cannot be improved upon, as Malone's gloss will show: 'sympathetick union of souls'[1] seems unnecessary, cumbersome and not even exact. For one thing, the word 'true' is partly metaphorical: true in the moral sense of faithful, constant, at one, but true also in the surveyor's sense, and the carpenter's and joiner's. Shakespeare's phrase is superior to Malone's because at every point it is closer to actual life; and 'marriage' is a much richer word than 'union', though it includes that meaning. 'Marriage', besides, leads forward to the 'impediments' of the next line (and here the commentators do well to recall the Marriage Service: 'If any of you know cause or just impediment why these two persons should not be joined together...').

Yet it is not primarily a poem about the *marriage* of true minds, for after the first line and a half marriage is not mentioned again. The real subject is true minds, the constancy of true love. And it is interesting to note, from the first line to the last, what a very negative poem it is.[2] Almost all its

---

[1] Quoted in Rollins, vol. I, p. 294.
[2] This was first pointed out to me by Betty Caplan, formerly of the University of Melbourne.

splendid and powerful affirmations are made in negative terms, or against a background of negation, destruction or change; and in its use of such a background, as in the pitch of its exaltation and in some of its phrasing and versification, it resembles Sonnet 55 ('Not marble, nor the guilded monuments'). The strong assertiveness of the first clause relies on negatives: 'Let me *not*... admit *impediments*'; when the definition of love begins in line 2, it takes a negative form: 'love is *not* love'; and this is followed by the virtual negatives of 'alter', 'bend' and 'remove'. The next quatrain's first positive assertion, 'it is an ever fixed marke', is introduced with 'O no', and the 'marke' must withstand, or calmly gaze on, the flux and tempests of the sea, and yet be 'never shaken'. In the next image, when love becomes a star, it stands in contrast to the '*wandring* barke' (uncontrolled, off its true course), and while the star's 'higth' can be taken, its 'worth' is still 'unknowne'. So, too, with the third quatrain: its positive and tremendous force comes in part through negatives. 'Lov's *not* Times *foole*', even though Time mows down the flowers of 'lips and cheeks'; again, love '*alters not*' with the seasons, but 'beares it out' (the phrase has a strong sense of overcoming obstacles, of enduring) 'even to the edge of doome'; and this again is something negative, the final abyss where all will sink and end. Nor does the couplet change the prevailing terms: it speaks of 'error', and its second line is emphatically and trebly negative:

> I *never* writ, *nor no man* ever loved.

Yet the poem's total effect is, of course, strongly positive: this is a poem of *negative assertions*, and it is worth pausing to ask how this comes to be so, how indeed the negatives get there in the first place. The speaker, I think, is stating his convictions about love not only in the face of the great obstacles he knows it must overcome (time, death, human frailty, and so on) but against the implied cynicism, concerning love, of someone else: the whole 'wise world', perhaps, of Sonnet 71. A charge has been made against love, and the poet is speaking as counsel for the defence, so it is natural that his denial of the charge will be partly couched in negative terms. What lends strength to this reading is the poem's frequent use of legal words, whether ecclesiastical ('impediments') or civil: 'admit' in line 2 is clearly a word of this kind, and according to Tucker[1] the second-last line calls up the same kinds of association. Of its first half, 'If this be error', he writes: 'The legal sense of "error" as a fault in a judgment is here entirely apt. Cf. "writ of errors".' And of the second half, 'upon me proved': 'i.e. if it is proved against me (and in my own case) that I have given an erroneous judgment in what I have just written.'

Much of the poem's strength comes from the simple, direct, largely monosyllabic diction noted by Tucker Brooke, and from the firm masculine voice of the poetry, as flexible as it is strong. There is never the slightest hint of monotony. Notice the variety of tone and movement, the run, rallentando, pause and broadening change of tempo here:

> love is not love
> Which alters when it alteration findes,
> Or bendes with the remover to remove.
> O no, it is an ever fixed marke.

And in the much-quoted line 9, 'Lov's not Times foole, though rosie lips and cheeks', the first four words are given almost equal weight (and weight is the word), recalling and even bettering the 'Shall you pace forth' of Sonnet 55; in

[1] *The Sonnets of Shakespeare*, ed. T. G. Tucker (Cambridge, 1924), p. 193.

this arresting stroke, technical virtuosity answers to the imaginative purpose: the effect must be of a voice firm and tolling with conviction; and the rest of the line, by contrast, trips off with hardly any stress, is almost thrown away, which again is imaginatively right.

The poem communicates directly, even at points where editors do well to gloss. Lines 7 and 8 use words with special as well as common meanings: 'marke', 'worth', 'higth...taken'. 'Marke', meaning sea-mark, is no trouble: the context explains it. Of the others, Tucker says: 'An astrological term followed by an astronomical. The "height" of a star is its angular altitude; this the mariner may "take" with his instruments. Its "worth" is its powers as an "influence"' (pp. 192-3). Yet along with their technical meanings the words have familiar connotations which are themselves relevant – and sufficient, I think, to give us the general sense. 'Marke', 'worth' and 'higth' all convey notions of spiritual or moral value by reference to the material world. We might also note the manner in which a double value is given to 'star': by the quick shift from the mysterious influence of the stars in astrology to the aid they give to the steersman, love is shown as a powerful guide from afar on both the practical and the meta-physical planes. It is a star to steer by, but its power is 'unknown'.

Other verbal effects should be noted. To test the power of the word 'bends' in line 4, for instance, turn to a typical gloss on the line: 'Or inclines, when one of the pair is un-faithful or turns away, to do the same thing'.[1] Or this, which gets much nearer: 'either (1) yields from firm erect-ness, or (2) swerves aside'.[2] But 'bends' conveys still more strongly, through its physical associations (a reed bowed

[1] Seymour-Smith, p. 169.   [2] Tucker, p. 192.

by the wind, for example), the weakening of the spirit which the line renders. Then, when the word recurs in line 10, it has an altogether different force. 'Bending sickle' means first of all 'curving sickle', a visual impression, but the word suggests the physical in other ways. Considered as a verb it is both transitive and intransitive: the sickle bends, that is, stoops towards its work; and also it bends the flowers, laying them low. Here it has something of the sense which Daniel gives it:

> When thou surcharg'd with burthen of thy yeeres,
> Shalt bend thy wrinkles homeward to the earth.[1]

So that we have in Shakespeare's line a multiple image of a bent blade bending to bend the flowers to their fate.[2] Next, from 'within his. . . sickles compasse', we get both the abstract sense of 'compass' and the suggestion, too, of a physical compass sweeping its arc, within which the flowers fall. And here we may briefly comment on 'rosie lips and cheeks': they are flowerlike, stylized emblems of beauty and youth, whether male or female; 'the prettiness', as Wilson Knight observes, 'underlining a fragility, almost a triviality'.[3]

This prompts a glance at the element of 'mutability' in the poem, and here we are brought back to the starting point: to the frequent negatives of one kind or another throughout. Time's scythe mows down beauty, and time itself is no more than a few 'breefe houres and weekes',

[1] Samuel Daniel, Delia, Sonnet XLII, in Poems and A Defence of Rhyme, ed. Arthur Colby Sprague (Chicago, 1965), p. 31.
[2] Professor L. C. Knights has suggested to me a similar multiple image in Hopkins. 'Flesh falls within sight of us, we, though our flower the same,/ Wave with the meadow, forget that there must/The sour scythe cringe, and the blear share come.' (The Wreck of the Deutschland). 'Cringe', as Professor Knights says, 'gives both the obsequious movement of the scythe and the cringing of the human grass that is mown'.
[3] The Mutual Flame, p. 123.

which will recall Donne's reference, in a similar context, to 'houres, dayes, moneths, which are the rags of time'. Men change also: lovers 'remove' though love does not. And then too, in this connection, we must notice how space is used, in the images of 'marke', 'star', 'wandring barke' and 'edge of doome'.[1] Here the 'wandring barke' is the central image. Considered against the vast spaces of the sea, any ship may seem to be wandering, especially without sea-mark or polestar. If the lines are spoken:

> O no, it is an ever fixed marke
> That lookes on tempests and is never shaken;
> It is the star to every wandring barke,

one will hear in the third an upward inflexion which is peculiarly moving. The line looks up, the voice rises, to the word 'star' and is held there for an instant by the long vowel. While this is part of the beauty of the line, it is only momentary: the voice is carried on, and the accents de-manded by the last part of the line, the measuring-out of stress on their sound and meaning ('to every wandring barke'), create at least half of the line's powerful and mixed emotion. Joy and sorrow, or perhaps compassion, blend. But not romantically, as in the early Yeats: 'And all the burden of her labouring ships'; it is much more controlled and subtle. The line insists both on the star and on the ship's wandering. The image is, of course, a stock Petrarchan one (see Wyatt's free translation from Petrarch: 'My galy charged with forgetfulnes':[2] the lover is a storm-tossed ship and 'The starres be hid'). But Shakespeare, as usual, is not merely repeating the received metaphor: it feels utterly different here, partly because love has now become so stable, so utterly and eternally dependable (no longer the tyran-

[1] Hallett Smith, *Elizabethan Poetry*, p. 175.
[2] Sir Thomas Wyatt, *Poems*, ed. Kenneth Muir (London, 1949), p. 22.

nous feudal Lord of love), but more especially because the metaphor has been generalized. '*Every* wandring barke': it is not just one wanderer we have to feel for, but each individual one among many, and the sea is that of all time, for it is an immutable love we are asked to contemplate. Yet while from one point of view Shakespeare generalizes, he also holds us to the particular, as the phrase shows: 'every', not 'all', a fine but real distinction. By being made both particular and general in this way the metaphor most easily engages our emotions: to each of us the bark represents himself and every other solitary wanderer. The imagery, while it suggests certain stable points, combines to create a sense of great height, immensities of space and darkness, the ship's uncertainty and frailty. It is this, I think, that gives pathos to the line; and all the more so as the reader's natural impulse to identify himself with the ship is so powerfully if briefly stimulated.

This is a poem which never falters, not even in its couplet, as some otherwise powerful sonnets do. It is what it must be if it is to persuade us: a resonantly certain statement of the certitudes of love. It is a poem – and what is more, a sonnet – without a flaw.

The two others I want to look at, more briefly, are equally well known, and will help to show the peculiar strengths of the love Shakespeare has to declare. First, Sonnet 73:

> That time of yeeare thou maist in me behold,
> When yellow leaves, or none, or few doe hange
> Upon those boughes which shake against the could,
> Bare ruin'd quiers, where late the sweet birds sang.
> In me thou seest the twi-light of such day,
> As after Sun-set fadeth in the West,
> Which by and by blacke night doth take away,
> Deaths second selfe that seals up all in rest.
> In me thou seest the glowing of such fire,

That on the ashes of his youth doth lye,
As the death bed, whereon it must expire,
Consum'd with that which it was nurrisht by.
  This thou percev'st, which makes thy love more strong,
  To love that well, which thou must leave ere long.

The sonnet, and its imagery, have been much discussed; all I shall do here is to stress again the extreme tranquillity of the self-abnegation. There is no wrenching, no effort, no despair: instead, a resignation precisely defined by its statement in terms of inexorable natural processes – those of the change of seasons, of night's coming after day, of the dying of a fire. Yet one has only to think of Hardy to see that such comparisons need not be free from a melancholy fatalism, however powerful. There is nothing of that here: no trace of complaint, or even of lament, that has not been transmuted into an extraordinary, disciplined stillness of spirit. Nor does the final couplet break down either emotionally or artistically. It is in the form of a statement, and though it is no doubt partly an appeal, there is nothing embarrassing about it, no self-pity, no naked and painful demand on the beloved.

It is of poems like this that C. S. Lewis's words seem most apt. Whatever its beginning, he says, Shakespeare's love ends by being 'the quintessence of all loves whether erotic, parental, filial, amicable, or feudal... The love is, in the end, so simply and entirely love that our *cadres* are thrown away and we cease to ask what kind... The greatest of the sonnets are written from a region in which love abandons all claims.'[1] *Some* of the greatest, anyhow; and these include my final example, Sonnet 71:

Noe Longer mourne for me when I am dead,
Then you shall heare the surly sullen bell

[1] *English Literature in the Sixteenth Century*, p. 505.

Give warning to the world that I am fled
From this vile world with vildest wormes to dwell:
Nay if you read this line, remember not,
The hand that writ it, for I love you so,
That I in your sweet thoughts would be forgot,
If thinking on me then should make you woe.
O if (I say) you looke upon this verse,
When I (perhaps) compounded am with clay,
Do not so much as my poore name reherse;
But let your love even with my life decay.
    Least the wise world should looke into your mone,
    And mocke you with me after I am gon.

It is easy to see why one reader I know should speak of this poem's 'immeasurable perfection'. It breathes the most complete and noble selflessness, and speaks in accents of extraordinary and profound simplicity ('remember not,/The hand that writ it, for I love you so...'). Yet it is not always read in this spirit, strangely enough. According to Martin Seymour-Smith (p. 149): 'This poem was written in a mood of such deep depression that it achieves an effect of quite gay sarcasm... The suggestion [in lines 12–14] is that the youth's love is so absurdly slight that any post-mortem on it would be received with mockery.' There *is* some sarcasm, but 'gay' it is not. Nor is it directed at the beloved. And that 'suggestion' claimed for the last lines is simply not there. Surely the poem is not saying: Forget me as soon as I'm dead – though I hardly need give you the advice, because you will anyway. Such a reading runs counter to the whole tone of the poem. I would, of course, agree that the tone is mixed. There is bitterness as well as love, but the bitterness is all for the 'wise' world, which has been stated at its true valuation in the 'vile' world of the first quatrain. There can be no question of two simultaneous voices here, two opposed meanings, as in Sonnet 57. The majestic and sorrowful opening lines, with their sonorous vowels ('Noe Longer mourne', 'surly sullen bell', 'give warning to the world'), can be read in only one way, and they establish the key for the whole poem. If there is any change it is to the heartfelt simplicity of the lines quoted earlier, and to the more open and bitter contempt for the world in the final couplet. And that bitterness must be seen as inseparable from the love professed. It would be wrong to think, as casual readers sometimes do, that the poem is 'beautiful' in a straightforward Victorian way: its emotion is far from simple. But on the other hand it is a unified emotion. Its complexity, as Murray Krieger points out,[1] is seen in the advice to do as the world does and so to give it no grounds for criticism of the beloved: advice which the poet would give only if prompted by love, and because he sees what kind of world the beloved must continue to live in after the poet's death.

It is quite impossible to consider all the statements on love which the Sonnets make: that would mean going through almost every poem in the sequence. My purpose has been to look at a few of the chief poems in detail, in order to show the particular poetic life given to the material in each. For the life of the poetry is of course what matters. But from the examples chosen the extraordinary *nature* of the love expressed should be perfectly clear. It is easy enough to see why C. S. Lewis should say that 'In certain senses of the word "love", Shakespeare is not so much our best as our only love poet' (p. 505). Certainly no one else, not even his nearest rival Donne, has given expression to such states as we see embodied in the poems discussed here, and in numerous others besides.

[1] *A Window to Criticism*, pp. 118–21.

4

The Sonnet and the Sonneteers

At this point it seems natural to look at some of the other love poetry of Shakespeare's time. In this chapter I shall consider, first of all, why so many English Renaissance poets chose to use the sonnet form and what use they made of it, and then go on to consider what sort of love we find represented by the chief sonneteers. Something must be said, too, of Ralegh, though other important love poetry, Marlowe's *Hero and Leander* and the songs of Ben Jonson, will be passed over without comment. I must confine the discussion to that body of love poetry which in some significant way acknowledges the Petrarchan convention; and this includes some of the *Songs and Sonets* of Donne, who will be discussed beside Shakespeare in the next chapter. Even though we may not feel Shakespeare's Sonnets to be strongly Petrarchan in character, or Donne's love poetry either, it is against that convention (as I have suggested already) that we can best see them. Indeed they invite us to do so, as Ben Jonson's love poems, for instance, do not.

Why the sonnet?

We might well ask, to begin with, why the sonnet form was chosen so often, or indeed at all; and in particular why Shakespeare should have chosen it, since among his unusually large body of sonnets comparatively few are perfect.

Why, then, the sonnet? I am not sure that a complete answer can be given. It will not do to say that sonneteering was a fashion which caught on after (and because of) the publication of *Astrophel and Stella*. There must have been something beyond even Sidney's tremendous influence as a literary figure, something attractive in the form itself. Not all poets, as we know, have felt it. 'Personally', wrote Edward Thomas, 'I have a dread of the sonnet. It must contain fourteen lines, and a man must be a tremendous poet or a cold mathematician if he can accommodate his thoughts to such a condition.'[1] And this, if anything, underrates the difficulties of the form. If fourteen lines were the only requirement, there would have been more successes than there are; and to judge from many sonnets of the 1590s, some of Shakespeare's among them, Ben Jonson was at least partly right to compare the sonnet to the bed of Procrustes, 'wher some who were too short were racked; and others too long cut short'.[2] In his own epigram 'On Lucy Countess of Bedford' a possible corrective to this danger is demonstrated. Like a Shakespearean sonnet this poem is composed of quatrains and a couplet, but it has four quatrains instead of three, and retains much of the feeling of a sonnet without yielding to the temptation to cut its idea down to less than size:

> This morning, timely rapt with holy fire,
> I thought to forme unto my zealous Muse,
> What kinde of creature I could most desire,
> To honor, serve, and love; as Poets use.
> I meant to make her faire, and free, and wise,
> Of greatest bloud, and yet more good then great;
> I meant the day-starre should not brighter rise,

---

[1] Quoted in J. W. Lever, *The Elizabethan Love Sonnet*, p. 162.
[2] Ben Jonson, *Conversations with William Drummond of Hawthornden*, in Ben Jonson, *Works*, ed. C. H. Herford and Percy Simpson (Oxford, 1954), vol. I, p. 134.

Nor lend like influence from his lucent seat.
I meant shee should be curteous, facile, sweet,
Hating that solemne vice of greatnesse, pride;
I meant each softest vertue, there should meet,
Fit in that softer bosome to reside.
Onely a learned, and a manly soule
I purpos'd her; that should, with even powers,
The rock, the spindle, and the sheeres controule
Of destinie, and spin her owne free houres.
Such when I meant to faine, and wish'd to see,
My Muse bad, *Bedford* write, and that was shee.[1]

Yet plainly there is something that called poets back to the sonnet again and again, whatever form of it they settled for; it had no serious rival. What was its appeal? Perhaps that it offered a mode of poetic thought which required discipline to be done well, and produced a shape (as M.M. Mahood suggests) which 'should communicate feeling, but feeling purified by being fully and finally comprehended'; the result being 'a satisfying organisation of sound and sense that conveys the ordered movement of thought into which the emotion has been shaped'.[2] This is an effect which the Renaissance poet seems very likely to have sought. No doubt he could have found it in other forms, but not in such full measure. In Renaissance prose, too, something very close to sonnet-structure is sometimes to be found; in this passage from Machiavelli, for instance:

When we consider the general respect for antiquity, and how often – to say nothing of other examples – a great price is paid for some fragments of an antique statue, which we are anxious to possess to ornament our houses with, or to give to artists who strive to imitate them in their own works; and when we see, on the other hand, the wonderful examples which the history of ancient kingdoms and republics presents to us, the prodigies of virtue and of wisdom dis-

[1] *Poems of Ben Jonson*, ed. GB. Johnston (London, 1954), p. 36.
[2] *Shakespeare's Wordplay*, p. 103.

played by the kings, captains, citizens, and legislators who have sacrificed themselves for their country, – when we see these, I say, more admired than imitated, or so much neglected that not the least trace of this ancient virtue remains, we cannot but be at the same time as much surprised as afflicted.[1]

Undoubtedly, too, the sonnet form offers a combination of advantage and challenge. 'The abstract sonnet pattern', as W.P. Ker says, 'turns in the mind of the sonneteer to a fresh new measure according to an old rule and measure.'[2] The form may give 'just that variety and unity which is the secret of life. The sonnet fails when it is monotonous. The sonnet is not a mere stanza; it is at least a double thing, with position in it and contradiction. It is a true argument.'[3] The precision of the form, the flexibility it gave within strict limits, the need to avoid monotony and insignificance (for, as Saintsbury says, 'there is nothing quite so null as an insignificant sonnet'):[4] these are some of the stimuli the form must have offered the poet, as indeed it does today.

But then there are the differences between the English and the Italian forms (and differences within the English). In some ways it is surprising that Shakespeare should have adopted the form which now bears his name, since it is the least subtle and least intricate of all the variants used by English poets. The Petrarchan sonnet, I think, is more demanding than any of these, and its rewards would seem likely to be greater. Despite this, it was in the 'Shakespearean' form that Shakespeare himself and one or two others wrote some of the finest sonnets in the language. So it may seem perverse to speak of the inferiority of the

[1] Niccolo Machiavelli, *The Discourses* (New York, 1950), pp. 103–4. I am indebted to my colleague D.C. Muecke for this example.
[2] W.P. Ker, *Form and Style in Poetry* (London, 1928), p. 100.
[3] *Ibid.* p. 173.
[4] George Saintsbury, *History of English Prosody* (New York, 1961), vol. I, p. 304.

Shakespearean form. What must be stressed, however, is that success within it is more threatened and more precarious than in the Petrarchan. And certainly, if the Shakespearean sonnet is less demanding in one way, it is a good deal more so in another. Precisely because of the lack of linking rhyme between the quatrains, there is a danger that each quatrain will appear cut off from the others or related in too mechanical a fashion (often through parallel syntax), and that the poem as a whole will have too simple a structure: three successive quatrains, more or less self-contained, and then a final couplet. It is a commonplace, too, that the couplet may make a damaging conclusion, sometimes too pat, sometimes an anticlimax. As Miss Mahood points out, it 'is too brief to contain the entire counter-statement to the first three quatrains without giving the impression that the poet is trying to wrench the poem back on its course. If, however, the poet too anxiously anticipates the final turn of thought throughout the first twelve lines, the couplet loses its epigrammatic spring.'[1]

If we ask why Shakespeare used the form, it is not much help to be told by Bowyer Nichols that

The only explanation seems to be that he considered the form evolved by Surrey and other English poets to have on the whole for English practice the advantage. He judged, as we may believe, that the classic symmetry of the Petrarchan sonnet was in English too difficult of attainment, that it cramped invention, and imposed too many sacrifices and concessions; and that the artistic end could better be achieved in the inferior medium.[2]

Nor to be told by T.S. Eliot that 'the sonnet of Shakespeare is not merely such and such a pattern, but a precise

---

[1] *Shakespeare's Wordplay*, p. 104.
[2] Quoted in H.C. Beeching (ed.), *The Sonnets of Shakespeare* (Boston, 1904), p. xlix.

way of thinking and feeling';[1] for often in reading the Sonnets we feel this not to be so: great as so many of them are, even some of the greatest are flawed by a discrepancy between form and idea, and Jonson's remark about the Procrustean bed seems very apposite. One has at times a suspicion that the sonnet form was not the perfect one for what Shakespeare had to say but simply the nearest to hand, and that the results of his putting it into use are sometimes of the 'near-enough' kind rather than the complete fusion of matter and form that they should be.

Brief illustration of these shortcomings will have to suffice, and we need not go beyond well-known sonnets for examples. First, Sonnet 30 will show how the couplet can let a whole sonnet down.

> When to the Sessions of sweet silent thought,
> I sommon up remembrance of things past,
> I sigh the lacke of many a thing I sought,
> And with old woes new waile my deare times waste:
> Then can I drowne an eye (un-us'd to flow)
> For precious friends hid in deaths dateles night,
> And weepe a fresh loves long since canceld woe,
> And mone th'expence of many a vannisht sight.
> Then can I greeve at greevances fore-gon,
> And heavily from woe to woe tell ore
> The sad account of fore-bemoned mone,
> Which I new pay as if not payd before.
> > But if the while I thinke on thee (deare friend)
> > All losses are restord, and sorrowes end.

What Miss Mahood says of the couplet applies to this, though she herself defends the poem: the couplet here cannot effectively reverse the tendency of the previous twelve lines, and the impression it creates is perfunctory and rather trite. Many of the couplets, as G. Wilson Knight says, bring

---

[1] Quoted in Hilton Landry, *Interpretations in Shakespeare's Sonnets*, p. 141.

'a drop, not only in tension, since this is expected, but in quality of thought too'.[1] Yet often the appearance of trite-ness, of intellectual collapse, may conceal, as here, the fact that the couplet is being asked to do the work of the whole sestet of a Petrarchan sonnet, and it is very rarely that two lines can achieve the effect of six. As to the drop in quality of thought, it is worth remarking that this occurs most often in couplets which begin (as in 30) with 'But' or 'And yet', whereas many of the strong couplets begin with 'Therefore' or 'So'. In other words the weak couplets are generally those which seek to *reverse* the sonnet's previous direction of thought, while the strong ones recapitulate or extend it.

Next, to see malformations or inconsistencies in texture, we might take Sonnet 60 (which also suffers from a weak final couplet).

> Like as the waves make towards the pibled shore,
> So do our minuites hasten to their end,
> Each changing place with that which goes before,
> In sequent toile all forwards do contend.
> Nativity once in the maine of light,
> Crawles to maturity, wherewith being crown'd,
> Crooked eclipses gainst his glory fight,
> And time that gave, doth now his gift confound.
> Time doth transfixe the florish set on youth,
> And delves the paralels in beauties brow,
> Feedes on the rarities of natures truth,
> And nothing stands but for his sieth to mow.
> > And yet to times in hope, my verse shall stand
> > Praising thy worth, dispight his cruell hand.

Here all is well until the third quatrain, which is not closely enough related to the earlier two and which tries to do too much, thus upsetting the measure and proportion of the

---

[1] *The Mutual Flame*, p. 81.

poem.[1] Quatrain two is related to quatrain one by shared images of movement: waves towards a shore, minutes towards their end, sun and child each across its proper scene, the eclipse across both. (Miss Mahood's account[2] of the poem up to this point is useful and perceptive, particularly in its stress on the double image of 'sun' and 'child' achieved by the verb 'crawles' after 'nativity'.) The relations between first and second quatrains are daring but just; by contrast, those between second and third are more strained. Perhaps they are not meant to be made at all, but the general movement of the sonnet, including the syntactical, encourages us to think the third is to be taken as a parallel to the first and second, and this sets up an expectation of related imagery, which is then to be baffled: time 'transfixes', 'delves', 'feeds', 'mows'. Some but not all of these can be brought into relation with earlier images, and only with considerably greater effort. It may be, as Miss Mahood argues, that a new ingredient is being stirred into the mixture: the 'florish' being that of a pen as well as the blossom of a tree, and looking forward to the 'hand' of Time in the closing line. And this would help to set up quatrain three and the couplet as a fairly well-defined sestet in its own right. But even then the result will be rather mixed, as the verbs of the quatrain serve to show; and the couplet itself leaves us feeling unconvinced and disappointed.

These two sonnets are well known, and with some reason; I quote them to show how even the better sonnets can sometimes be defective. To set against these we might name Sonnet 55 ('Not marble, nor the guilded monuments'), which I shall discuss in a later chapter. It deserves

---

[1] J.W. Lever takes a different view of the poem in *The Elizabethan Love Sonnet*, pp. 248–55.
[2] *Shakespeare's Wordplay*, pp. 95–6.

mention here as a perfect sonnet, where the procession of quatrains and couplet is strong and unified, building what the poem calls itself, a 'powrefull rime'. And of the many poems, by Shakespeare and others, on the power of art to outlast time's ravages, this is one of the few to vindicate its claims by the very solidity with which it is made.

Indeed, as I have been suggesting, the question of whether the sonnet form is justified arises each time it is used, and in Shakespeare's case the answer to that question varies greatly from one sonnet to another. In some it seems to be quite definitely *not* the form the poetic idea required; in others the marriage could not have been a happier one. This variation might tell us something about the lesser sonneteers as well, and about the whole sonneteering industry of the 1590s. There seems to have been a general determination to *write sonnets*, regardless of the artistic consequences; and the regardlessness was greatest, of course, among the poets of smallest wit.

But in reading the work of the sonneteers one notices much more than the use of a verse form, even if this served them as a kind of banner. I must now consider more broadly their achievement as love poets.

Sidney, Daniel, Drayton, Spenser

In these sequences one is struck both by the importance of the Petrarchan convention as a framework, a central *datum*, and by the way in which its original significance is so often lost or debased. A situation, a set of images used by Petrarch to express real pain and exalted vision are now, time and again, treated perfunctorily, put to merely decorative purposes. And it is not only the poets themselves who seem less serious. Where Laura refused because she must, most of these mistresses are merely coy ('Come you pretty, false-eyed wanton', etc.). So there are changes here in the conception of love which the poetry offers, and there are also questions to be asked about the level of poetic intelligence displayed in each sequence. I shall have to ignore the host of lesser sonneteers, but at the head of this survey of the four chief figures other than Shakespeare, I want to place a poem by Ralegh. A fragment, and I think totally disregarded by critics, it is one of his finest pieces; the main reasons for quoting it here are that it recaptures some of the pristine qualities of the Petrarchan vision and that it shows the dignity which poetry written in this convention could still attain in the late sixteenth century. It comes closer than any other English poem I know to suggesting the grandeur of Petrarch's own idea of the mistress: for Ralegh, as for Petrarch,[1] she holds absolute sway over the powers of life and death. She is 'the sun', and the poetry restores to this traditional image its original and elemental force.

> My dayes delights, my springetyme ioies fordvnn,
> Which in the dawne, and risinge soonn of youth
> Had their creation, and weare first begunn,
>
> Do in the yeveninge, and the winter sadd,
> Present my minde, which takes my tymes accompt,
> The greif remayninge of the ioy it had.
>
> My tymes that then rann ore them sealves in thes,
> And now runn out in others happines,
> Bring vnto thos new ioyes, and new borne dayes.
>
> So could shee not, if shee weare not the soonn,
> Which sees the birth, and buriall, of all elce,
> And holds that poure, with which shee first begvnn;

[1] Petrarch, Sonnet, 'Quando 'l pianeta...', *Canzoniere* No. IX, ed. Michele Scherillo (Milan, 1908), pp. 9–10.

Levinge each withered boddy to be torne
By fortune, and by tymes tempestius,
Which by her vertu, once faire frute have borne,

Knowinge shee cann renew, and cann create
Green from the grovnde, and floures, yeven out of stone,
By vertu lastinge over tyme and date,

Levinge vs only woe, which like the moss,
Havinge cumpassion of vnburied bones
Cleaves to mischance, and vnrepayred loss.

For tendre stalkes —

(Unfinished)[1]

The plainness, sonority and strength of this are all too rare
in English Petrarchan poetry after Wyatt, and it is worth
stressing that this is one of the few poems of its time to
approach the resonant gravity and simplicity of some of
Shakespeare's sonnets: once more 'Noe Longer mourne for
me' comes to mind.

To move back from Ralegh's poem to Sidney's *Astrophel
and Stella* is of course to pass from a single incomplete lyric
to an ambitious and varied sequence, but a sequence which
one may find hard to read without some irritation. Its
historical importance, of course, is clear. It set the pattern
for the sequences which followed, where neither the lover
nor the mistress need be characterized in much detail and
where a love situation becomes the point of departure and
return for a variety of poetic excursions: meditations on
sleep or the lack of it, complaints written in absence from
the beloved, an apostrophe to her lapdog or her sparrow, or
to the moon, and, more seriously, reflections on time, death,
dissolution, immortality (and especially on that kind within

---

1 *The Poems of Sir Walter Ralegh*, ed. Agnes Latham (London, 1962), p. 44.

the poet's gift). Equally important, Sidney's sequence passes on a version of Petrarchan love which becomes standard:

> Then ev'n of fellowship, ô Moone, tell me
> Is constant *Love* deem'd there but want of wit?
> Are Beauties there as proud as here they be?
> Do they above love to be lov'd, and yet
>   Those Lovers scorne whom that *Love* doth possesse?
>   Do they call *Vertue* there ungratefulnesse?
>
> (Sonnet 31)[1]

And one must concede that Sidney makes some attempt here and there to give this situation an interesting life, as in those sonnets which deal with the conflict between reason and sense, desire and honour. This conflict finds its most interesting expression in the song beginning 'In a grove most rich of shade', quoted in chapter 3. (In passing, one might note that the songs interspersed among the sonnets give Sidney's sequence one of its most attractive features. It seems a pity they have no true counterparts in the other sequences I shall be discussing, though in a sense the great *Epithalamion* is the song that crowns Spenser's *Amoretti*.)

The main objection to Sidney's attempt, I think, is that finally it is trivial. He is often praised for brilliance, polish, courtly ease, but too often the reality fails to square with this. The intended lightness, in which the courtly ease ought to be found, is as a rule merely fatuous:

> Flie, fly, my friends, I have my death wound; fly,
> See there that boy, that murthring boy I say,
> Who like a theefe, hid in darke bush doth ly,
> Till bloudie bullet get him wrongfull pray.
>
> (Sonnet 20)

This kind of playfulness is one of the recurring features

---

[1] *The Poems of Sir Philip Sidney*, ed. William A. Ringler, Jr, p. 180. All references are to this edition.

which suggest in fact a *lack* of ease about the whole undertaking. Again and again this playfulness breaks in to blunt
the edge of the material, or the poetry finds other ways to
fritter or hide its potential strength. A vacuous exuberance
lights on conceits like this, for instance:

> I on my horse, and *Love* on me doth try
> Our horsmanships, while by strange worke I prove
> A horsman to my horse, a horse to *Love*
>
> (Sonnet 49)

or on the extended comparison of Stella's face ('Queene
Vertue's court') to a richly adorned palace (Sonnet 9). The
verse is often over-patterned and abstract: apart from some
passages of colloquial rhythm and diction, which seem more
like virtuoso mimicry than the real thing, there is much
reliance on intricate verbal linkings which, while pleasing
when used sparingly:

> *Stella*, the onely Planet of my light,
> Light of my life, and life of my desire,
> Chiefe good, whereto my hope doth only aspire,
> World of my wealth, and heav'n of my delight.
>
> (Sonnet 68)

can quickly become wearisome. In fact, isolated examples of
any of these features will hardly suggest their cumulative
effect in a reading of the whole sequence. There are of
course many moments of success (such as the famous ending
of the first sonnet: '"Foole," said my Muse to me, "looke
in thy heart and write."'); and the best sonnets, which are
fewer than we have been led to believe, do achieve a successful balance between the playful and the serious, the artful
and the inevitable. The much-quoted Sonnet 47 ('What,
have I thus betrayed my libertie?') illustrates this well.

It is easy to see why *Astrophel and Stella* inspired other

poets to attempt the same kind of thing, even if one must see too that it set a bad example in some ways, above all by taking most of the sting out of its central, Petrarchan, situation.

One measure of Sidney's achievement is that when we turn from him to Daniel our first impression is of the narrower range of Daniel's poetic ambitions. *Delia*, nevertheless, is marked by a greater ease, a more fluid musicality: whatever its limitations, it does sing, and often memorably. It can be fleet and graceful, 'though it be done but slightly' (Sonnet I). Yet, as so often happens, the anthology pieces turn out to contain the best of Daniel: poems like 'Carecharmer Sleepe' (XLV), with its almost Shakespearean music, and 'Faire is my Love' (VI). In the second of these, however, one notices a tell-tale prettifying of the mistress: there is not much of the Petrarchan severity left here, such as we do certainly find in Sidney's song, already referred to, as well as in Ralegh; not much, either, of the at once forbidding and tempting character of Wyatt's 'hind':

> *Noli me tangere*, for Cesars I ame;
> And wylde for to hold, though I seme tame.[1]

Nor, on the other hand, is there any trace of the relenting mistress of Wyatt's best-known poem. But instead:

> Faire is my loue, and cruell as sh'is faire;
> Her brow shades frownes, although her eyes are sunny;
> Her Smiles are lightning, though her pride dispaire;
> And her disdaines are gall; her fauours hunny.
> A modest maide, deckt with a blush of honour,
> Whose feete doe treade greene pathes of youth and loue,
> The wonder of all eyes that looke vppon her:
> Sacred on earth, design'd a Saint aboue.
> Chastitie and Beautie, which were deadly foes,
> Liue reconciled friends within her brow:
> And had she pittie to conioine with those,

[1] *Poems*, ed. Muir, p. 7.

Then who had heard the plaints I vtter now.
O had she not beene faire, and thus vnkinde,
My Muse had slept, and none had knowne my minde.

(Sonnet VI)[1]

Pleasant as this is, we can hardly believe in the mistress or in the poet's love for her. Is it enough that Daniel is 'making a poem', composing a variation on a well-known theme? If he doesn't take the passion seriously, will he persuade us to take its issue seriously either? The combination of the code-words 'fair', 'cruel', 'disdain', 'foes', 'pity', with the insipid, curiously middle-class suggestions of 'modest maid', 'blush of honour', 'green paths of youth and love' (and surely the rest of the poem queries the 'love'?), drains the blood out of the conventional material. The poem is a thoughtless one: Daniel's mind is not on the meanings of the words he is using, and the total effect, ensured by the final couplet, is unintentionally smug, and open to parody: It's a good thing she wouldn't have me, because now I have my poetry instead.[2]

Intellectually, then, the poetry is feeble. Melody is its aim, and banality, sometimes, its end. A poem like XI ('Teares, vowes, and prayers') spins out the little it has to say without disguising a meagre and essentially common-place idea. There is no attempt to 'make it new': the poetry does not explore, it embroiders. Which may be said of Daniel's sequence as a whole. The intellectual weakness is discernible even in the musical and metrical pattern; in the banal rhyming at the end of XLII, for instance:

But ah no more, thys hath beene often tolde,
And women grieue to thinke they must be old.

[1] Samuel Daniel, *Poems and A Defence of Rhyme*, ed. Arthur Colby Sprague, p. 13. All references are to this edition.
[2] 'The world should thank me for not marrying Willie Yeats' (Maud Gonne).

Though, to be fair, this sonnet contains some of Daniel's finest and most resonant verse, as in the lines which Shakespeare may have recalled in his Sonnet 116:

> When thou surcharg'd with burthen of thy yeeres,
> Shalt bend thy wrinkles homeward to the earth.

(And we have seen how weak some of Shakespeare's couplets can be.)

It may seem that this attack on Daniel is irrelevant, that his attitude to love is not the point. But a poet who takes up material about which he does not feel deeply must know how to handle it. No love poetry should strike us as Cowley's *Mistress* struck Johnson: as having been written 'for hire by a philosophical rhymer who had only heard of another sex'.[1] Though a poet need not take his subject completely seriously, he must see its implications, see all round it and all round his use of it. This Daniel does not succeed in doing: we miss the signs of a poetic intelligence aware, and making us aware, that where a passion might once have stood a delicate artifice is now being raised. Yet since much of Daniel's artifice is so pleasant, the last word on it must be of severe qualification rather than dismissal.

In Drayton there is rather more to admire. He is no more fired than Daniel by the passion of love, and in his address to his reader[2] he says so honestly, with something of the attitude of Shakespeare's 'plain man', who cannot heave his heart into his mouth and is therefore the more to be trusted. We are now in touch with a tougher poetry, with a robust, sardonic common sense, with a humour that can make a better job of the anecdotal conceit than Sidney could (*Idea*,

---

[1] 'Life of Cowley' in *Lives of the English Poets*, vol. I, p. 28.
[2] Sonnet 1, 'To the Reader of these Sonnets', in *Idea; in Sixtie Three Sonnets*, in *The Works of Michael Drayton*, ed. J. William Hebel (Oxford, 1961), vol. II, p. 310.

Sonnet 7), with a speaking rather than a singing voice, though it can sing too, on occasion. When he writes in the Petrarchan vein, as in Sonnet 26, 'To Despaire', the results are mediocre, but on the whole he avoids it. Three sonnets, in different kinds, should be singled out. 'To Time' (17), the least well known of the three, is a 'mutability poem' of exceptional lyrical dignity. It is a pity the poem has not been much noticed; it shows how well a minor poet could do in a great age.

> Stay, speedy Time, behold, before thou passe,
> From Age to Age, what thou hast sought to see,
> One, in whom all the Excellencies be,
> In whom, Heav'n lookes it selfe as in a Glasse:
> Time, looke thou too, in this Tralucent Glasse,
> And thy Youth past, in this pure Mirrour see,
> As the World's Beautie in his Infancie,
> What it was then, and thou before it was;
> Passe on, and to Posteritie tell this,
> Yet see thou tell, but truly, what hath beene:
> Say to our Nephewes, that thou once hast seene,
> In perfect humane shape, all heav'nly Blisse;
>   And bid them mourne, nay more, despaire with thee,
>   That she is gone, her like againe to see.

This, first published in 1594, cannot match Shakespeare in a similar vein, but does not look contemptible in his company. The other two sonnets are better known. The uneven but striking Sonnet 6, 'How many paltry, foolish, painted things', deserves notice as one of those poems which promise eternity to the beloved. At moments it treats this theme with some authority, in contrast to the mere gesture made by Daniel in 'Faire is my Love'. And Drayton's most celebrated sonnet, 'Since ther's no helpe, Come let us kisse and part' (Sonnet 61), shows what all his best poems show, that he knew how to learn from his contemporaries. 'Since ther's no helpe' must seem the most fully dramatic of Elizabethan sonnets until we realize that it is not Elizabethan at all. It was not added to the sequence until the last edition, published in 1619; Drayton had had time to learn from Elizabethan and Jacobean drama and (more important, I think) from the love poetry of Donne. He has applied the Donne technique to the love sonnet, and the result is a miniature dramatic love poem in which the form gives a neat, swift inevitability to the progression of the experience, or rather to the lover's argument: he begins by seeming to accept the parting but he so plays up the emotion, working on the mistress's feelings, that by the couplet it seems likely that there will be *no* parting after all.

If this poem suggests the work of other poets, the fact prompts two opposed judgments. On the one hand Drayton's poetry must seem limited by being derivative; on the other his awareness of what greater poets were doing was a means by which, during fifteen years or so, he strengthened his own work. If the example of great poets can be used to achieve a better and better kind of minor poetry, the results, as these three sonnets alone show, are worthwhile.

Turning to Spenser, we find ourselves for the first time in the presence of a master. The voice is unmistakeable, it is strong, it can be relied on always to be itself and challengingly so, and this is welcome even if the idiosyncrasies are sometimes bothering. Here indeed is a poet with some of the desired awareness of what he is doing: he is in charge of the undertaking in a way that the others are not, he has a vastly broader and more complete understanding of what it is all about, what the conventional framework can be made to contain. One is struck by the resourcefulness, the inventiveness, the variety, the power to grasp a poetic idea and carry it through. The verse is as musical as Daniel's but more consistent, and it rings with a more personal and compelling accent. This is a poet making the conventions his own; which means, among other things, extending them.

> After long stormes and tempests sad assay,
>> which hardly I endured heretofore:
>> in dread of death and daungerous dismay,
>> with which my silly barke was tossed sore:
> I doe at length descry the happy shore,
>> in which I hope ere long for to arryue;
>> fayre soyle it seems from far and fraught with store
>> of all that deare and daynty is alyue.
> Most happy he that can at last atchyue
>> the joyous safety of so sweet a rest:
>> whose least delight sufficeth to depriue
>> remembrance of all paines which him opprest.
> All paines are nothing in respect of this,
>> all sorrowes short that gaine eternall blisse.[1]

This is at once a version of du Bellay's 'Heureux qui, comme Ulysse...' and a turning of the Petrarchan story towards a happy ending: the storm-tossed bark is no longer 'despairing of the port'. It is, in part, by giving this new conclusion of Christian wedded love to the old story that Spenser shows his individuality.

And yet the *Amoretti* are marred by tiresome absurdities:

> But my proud one doth worke the greater scath,
>> through sweet allurement of her louely hew:
>> that she the better may in bloody bath
>> of such poore thralls her cruell hands embrew.

> (XXXI)

This, surely, is extravagantly remote from any imaginable dealings of lover and mistress, and it is not to the point to say that it is only a way of speaking: it is a ridiculous way of

---

[1] Spenser, *Amoretti* LXIII in *The Poetical Works of Edmund Spencer*, ed. J.C. Smith, and E. de Selincourt (Oxford, 1957), p. 573.

speaking. The memorable sonnets are either decorative pieces (pleasing as in XXVI, 'Sweet is the Rose', mechanically ornate as in XV, 'Ye tradefull Merchants'), or else they are 'immortalizations' such as LXXV, 'One day I wrote her name upon the strand' (which I shall discuss later), or such protestations as LXXXIIII:

> Let not one sparke of filthy lustfull fyre
>   breake out, that may her sacred peace molest:
>   ne one light glance of sensuall desyre
>   Attempt to work her gentle mindes vnrest.
> But pure affections bred in spotlesse brest,
>   and modest thoughts breathd from wel tempred sprites
>   goe visit her in her chast bowre of rest,
>   accompanyde with angelick delightes.
> There fill your selfe with those most ioyous sights,
>   the which my selfe could neuer yet attayne:
>   but speake no word to her of these sad plights,
>   which her too constant stiffenesse doth constrayn.
> Onely behold her rare perfection,
>   and blesse your fortunes fayre election.

Memorable, I said: yes, but also hard to take. We find here something characteristic of the Spenser of the *Amoretti* (and beyond): the accomplishment and polish of the verse, the exalted moral tone, combined with, and not quite masking, an attitude which has been well described as 'pervy'. The first line, with its lofty disavowals, has an air of protesting too much, and this is supported by much that follows. Apart from the cloying and suffocating nature of it all, one may catch oneself wondering about the state of mind which prompts such phrasing. The Donne of the *Elegies*, even the more savage of them, seems a more congenial figure: he, and the poetry itself, are at least honest. And even if the sentiments expressed in this sonnet are as admirably high-minded as they were intended to be, aren't they beside the point at this stage? The lover has won the mistress, and there seems no great harm in an occasional glance of 'sensuall desyre' towards one's Intended. The personality revealed by this poem, and by others, is one which idealizes, ornaments, strikes attitudes whether they are appropriate or not, and which cannot deal directly with experience, with selves and the real relationships between them.

*   *   *

What emerges from the discussion of these poets? A picture, I hope, of various talents, each yielding achievements we should not wish to be without, but talents whose limitations press upon us, more or less heavily, as we read the poetry: limitations at once of art and of vision. Sometimes it seems to be a limited view of art that has caused the limited view of experience, though one cannot be certain of this. It may, rather, be a lack of personality in the poet, and, following from that, a willingness to take refuge in the too-easy use of a verse form, and of a whole convention, without re-thinking or re-experiencing. Once the sonneteering craze caught on, the sonnet was a form ready-to-hand, one which could tempt even the stronger poets to use it whether the poetic material demanded it or not.

As for the Petrarchan convention, it is clear that few of the poets took its central situation very seriously. Ralegh did, and showed what lay at its core for the poet who could discover it. Sidney, too, hinted at this, and at the implicit moral conflicts, but he made too little of these, and the pattern he handed on to those who imitated him, the example he set them of how to view love and how to put a sonnet sequence together, seems to have been disabling as well as inspiring. None of the four poets, not even Spenser, gives us a strong sense of reality. What that is, I hope the next chapter will show.

The Petrarchan convention, like any other, can become dead and useless; it is just as alive, just as fruitful of poetic meaning as the poet can make it. Or to put this differently, there is life to be found in it and life to be brought to it. The finding and the bringing both depend on the individual poet. Sidney suggested a wide range of possibilities without exploring their depths; Daniel brought and found very little, but sang sweetly at the fountain-side; Drayton wisely saw that he and the convention could do little for each other and took his own path to a modest good fortune. Spenser is the one major poet we have encountered, but in the field of the love sonnet his achievement, too, is limited: a commanding accent, certainly, but not the sense of reality we get from the greatest love poets, nor the high degree of poetic intelligence which alone can bring that sense of reality into artistic being. These are the qualities we find so fully present in the two great poets we can turn to, finally, now.

5

Shakespeare and Donne

With Shakespeare and Donne the focus shifts, from poets working for the most part *within* a convention to poets who are aware of it, use it, criticize it in the broadest and profoundest terms, and transcend it completely. Free of any limits it may have imposed on the vision and language of lesser poets, even of a great but still a lesser poet like Spenser, they can employ it as part of much larger imaginative schemes than the others ever dreamed of. Shakespeare and Donne are, as Patrick Cruttwell says, 'incomparably the greatest English poets' of their time and 'in some vital respects akin to each other'.[1] Their kinship, so far as love poetry and this chapter are concerned, can be seen in more than one way: negatively, in their similar critiques of contemporary poetic love, and positively, in the kind of love they affirmed, the shared sense of selfhood and of relationship in the experience of love. But along with these similarities go marked differences. I am not thinking of stature: Shakespeare is obviously a greater and an ampler poet than Donne, but in the field of love poetry the difference in stature is less noticeable, and even, I think, disappears. The chief differences are in poetic temperament, and these must be discussed later in the chapter. For the moment it is enough to point out that even in these they are complementary, like the phoenix and turtle, the eagle and the dove,

[1] *The Shakespearean Moment*, p. xi.

and that it is from within this complementary relationship that they crown their age.

I have already suggested that Shakespeare's Sonnet 130 ('My Mistres eyes are nothing like the Sunne') is both a clever piece of literary satire and an affirmation of the dark woman's unconventional yet very real attractiveness: she is 'as rare,/As any she beli'd with false compare'. This poem serves as a useful starting-point for the discussion of both poets, for it touches on the assumptions about art and about experience on which their love poetry is based.

In Shakespeare's case it is not only in this sonnet (and, less obviously, in others) but in the plays as well that we see his amused and discerning awareness of Petrarchan excess. In Donne we find a similar awareness, and a similar use, of conventional material. If we are less conscious of it, and more surprised when it is pointed out, this is because of the impact made by Donne's highly individual poetic personality. There is nothing like it among his contemporaries; even Shakespeare, in the Sonnets, is closer in accent and manner to the other sonneteers.

Donne's poetry, in fact, sounds so original that we can easily forget how conventional it is, how much it uses the conventions it also mocks. Donne has a way of making everything he touches look new and absolutely his own, even when it is not. And Helen Gardner's recent edition of his love poems[1] quite properly draws attention to some of the things he borrowed, or (to follow Eliot) stole. Even the famous compasses, it seems, may have been made in Italy. No one would suppose this mattered, of course, except as one of the many signs that Donne was alive to the poetry being written around him. But while we give notional

---

[1] *The Elegies and the Songs and Sonnets of John Donne*, ed. Helen Gardner (Oxford, 1965).

assent to this, and to his awareness of the Petrarchan convention in particular, we do not always read individual poems in the light of what we know, and sometimes as a result we miss the point.

'Twicknam Garden' is an example of this. It is often taken to express a deeply-felt personal anguish, caused presumably by a hopeless passion for Lucy, Countess of Bedford. Sometimes an element of self-mockery is detected also, but the voice of the lover is still assumed to be the voice of Donne. This reading, I think, is mistaken. 'Twicknam Garden' is above all a comic poem, where the lover and the poet are not to be identified; a poem which exists not to give vent to Donne's feelings but to dramatize a certain perception about Petrarchan love. In calling it comic I am not of course denying either its seriousness or its grave beauty. But its eye is a satirical one, and the satire is at once literary and psychological. Like 'My Mistres eyes are nothing like the Sunne', the poem turns a clear-eyed, reducing gaze on the more foolish kinds of Petrarchan extravagance and offers instead a quite extra-conventional sense of reality; but its strategy is more oblique and its enquiry more searching, and this, along with the strong sense of individuality, may be why it is so frequently misread.

A.J. Smith, in some remarks in his small book on the *Songs and Sonets*, is one of the few critics to have seen its true aim.[1] He finds the poem 'a huge high-comic hyperbole' and the speaker's tone that of 'a man who is not likely to take his attitudinising too seriously, or his subject either'. Again, in speaking of the typical Petrarchan lover, who 'recognizes his grim plight but is powerless to amend it while his heart rules his judgment', Smith remarks that 'a poem like *The Blossome* seems precisely cast to demonstrate

[1] A.J. Smith, *John Donne: The Songs and Sonets* (London, 1964), pp. 50–1.

the *unmanliness* of such deeply committed subservience
as that' (p. 51; the italics are mine). And this would seem
to be a very apt description of 'Twicknam Garden' also;
more apt, indeed, than any talk of self-mockery, which
keeps us too close to the assumption that the speaker is the
poet. Donne is certainly mocking someone, but not, I think,
himself. His poem is virtually a dramatic monologue, and
not his only one after all: 'The Apparition', admittedly a
cruder poem, is another. The shocking immediacy with
which it renders the lover's imaginings may conceal at
first what Donne is offering: not a confession, but a new
dramatic treatment of material which Wyatt, for example,
had used in 'My lute awake' and which Campion, possibly
latest of the three, handled in 'When thou must home to
shades of underground'. Donne seems to have said: Let me
see if I can re-animate this figure. In 'Twicknam Garden'
he has done the same, but with far more resonance and
subtlety. This time the figure is that of the Petrarchan lover
in a spring garden, and the situation is derived, as Smith
reminds us, from Petrarch's own much-imitated '*Zefiro
torna*'. Once more taking a stock figure and situation,
Donne asks: What is it really like to be in that state? What
does it do to a man?

There is little need to rehearse the other passages where
Donne refers, dismissively, to the Petrarchans. In 'Loves
Growth', for instance:

> Love's not so pure, and abstract, as they use
> To say, which have no Mistresse but their Muse.[1]

And in 'The Canonization':

---

[1] The text of Donne's poems used throughout is that of H. J. C. Grierson,
2 vols. (Oxford, 1912), though I have also consulted Helen Gardner's
edition, already referred to.

> What merchants ships have my sighs drown'd?
> Who saies my teares have overflow'd his ground?

And again, more gently, in the 'Valediction: forbidding mourning':

> No teare-floods, nor sigh-tempests move,
> T'were prophanation of our joyes
> To tell the layetie our love.

'Twicknam Garden' begins with the same pair of images, 'Blasted with sighs, and surrounded with teares', as much as to say: Enter the conventional lover. There is no open derision yet, though 'blasted' and 'surrounded' both hint that the speaker has a generous sense of his own misery. Primarily the imagery is used as a tag to identify the particular variety of the speaker; and admittedly the next three lines seem to work counter to any comic effect:

> Hither I come to seeke the spring,
> And at mine eyes, and at mine eares,
> Receive such balmes, as else cure every thing.

It is not until the second half of the stanza that the implications of the opening are taken up and extended:

> But O, selfe traytor, I do bring
> The spider love, which transubstantiates all,
> And can convert Manna to gall,
> And that this place may thoroughly be thought
> True Paradise, I have the serpent brought.

Here is a lover who broods lovingly on his pain, shuddering deliciously and not to be deterred from the most grandiose comparisons. The prolonged, almost masochistic wit of these lines, while it is carefully worked out by the poet, suggests a disorder, a loss of the sense of proportion on the part of his persona. We can only accept it completely if the poem offers it on these terms. Already in this stanza we notice the complete poetic control which is to be found throughout: a flexible firmness in the verse, a marvellously intricate, grave dance in the rhyme-scheme and the metrical pattern (with longer and shorter lines interchanging). This control stands as a witness to the order of the poem, as against the turmoil of the lover's feelings.

His obsessive self-concern becomes more marked in the second stanza: winter should, for him, 'benight the glory of this place', and the upside-downness of this demand is given sly and ludicrous emphasis by the word 'wholsomer'. The paranoia comes into the open with 'forbid/These trees to laugh, and mocke mee to my face'. This is not the language of self-mockery but of a mind too self-concerned to be capable of that. Yet here again everything about the verse suggests an assured imaginative grasp. The second half of the stanza intensifies the impression of a lover driven beyond measure and self-respect, unable either to bear the mockery of the garden or to stop loving, and so prepared to become something 'senslesse'. We should be struck, as he perhaps is not, by the 'unmanliness' of this: he is so much reduced, so much less than a man, that he is willing to become a mandrake or a stone fountain, choosing the two lowest rungs of the ladder of being, and even these in descending order.

I would certainly agree that the end of this stanza is, in a beautiful poem, particularly beautiful: an effect compounded of the gravity of the cadences, the ingenuity of the conceits, and the manner in which the objects (mandrake groaning, stone fountain weeping) express and stylize the lover's emotion with the calm of mimetic art. But as with Yeats' golden bird there is something incongruous and absurd about them: the beauty, being a matter of artifice instead of humanity, is finally a joke. The poetry is magnificently comprehensive here: the genuine beauty the lover imagines even in his absurdity is taken up into the poem's larger design, and yet the implications never cease to be comic ones.

It is the same with the opening of stanza three:

> Hither with christall vyals, lovers come,
>   And take my teares, which are loves wine,
>   And try your mistresse Teares at home.

Again the formal pavane-like movement, the verbal evocation of a grave, delicate ritual; beautiful, beyond any doubt, but how comic the beauty is, with its fantastic elaborations. The lovers are to come with their little flasks and take away samples of his tears, for experimental purposes, it would seem. ('*Try* your mistresse Teares': at a sort of wine-tasting? in a court of law, or of love? in the laboratory?). There follows a sudden outburst: 'For all are false, that tast not just like mine', where the paranoia reaches its climax; and then a kind of exhausted lull ('Alas, hearts do not in eyes shine', etc.) while the emotion gathers itself together for another howl of pain: 'O perverse sexe, where none is true but shee'. And the verbal contortions of the final paradox catch nicely the inner contortions of the half-crazed lover. It is part of the effect, too, that the poem should end with a stress (dictated not only by rhyme but by the weight of the final line) on the first-person pronoun:

> O perverse sexe, where none is true but shee,
>   Who's therefore true, because her truth kills mee.

This, then, is a critique of Petrarchan love, an attack not so much on a way of writing as on the nature of the feeling it claimed to represent. Nor does it stand alone in Donne's work: it is merely the most sustained treatment of a subject which recurs again and again. And to see it as a personal poem, with or without the self-mockery, is a poor compliment, I think, both to Donne's powers of self-knowledge and to his art. On the one hand we have to see him as a besotted fool; on the other we have to ignore the poetry.

But could it still somehow be argued that he wrote the poem because, deeply in love with Lady Bedford, he found himself in the same plight as the conventional lover? That under cover of writing a conventional poem he was really writing a very personal one? That the poem is in fact a 'double bluff'? Possibly; but surely it is too much trouble? We could speculate endlessly about the poem's role (if any) in the relationship (whatever it was). He was in love with her and knew his case to be hopeless, as Petrarch's was, so he chose a Petrarchan mask to tell her of his plight, and, what is more, meant every word he said, but the mask saved his face for him (and perhaps hers as well). Or, he was not in love with her, but others thought he was, which was a joke he shared with her, so he assumed poetically the role people had assigned to him, and wrote her the standard complaint. These and other theories are entertaining, but needn't be entertained. There *is* just the faintest possibility that Donne meant the poem to be read 'straight', but even if we disregard the qualities of the poem itself, it is unlikely that such an acute poet would be writing a straight Petrarchan poem at that point in time; far more likely that he was making a beautifully comic *exposé* of the normal Petrarchan heart.

To see all this more clearly, we might 'try' the poem against the 'Nocturnall upon S. Lucies Day', where, if some of the ingredients are the same, the taste is noticeably different. Probably we should resist the temptation to think that the poet's own feelings are involved. This, after all, may well be another illusion: we are still dealing with a dramatic poem, and 'I did best', Donne said himself, 'where

I had least truth for my subjects'. But certainly it is harder in this poem to measure, or even detect, the distance between poet and persona; and the persona is neither a conventional lover nor subject to the poet's mockery. Helen Gardner and others have rightly found similarities here to 'Twicknam Garden', chiefly in the lover's dejection and in some of his imagery: 'Yea plants, yea stones detest,/And love'; 'yet all these seeme to laughe,/Compar'd with mee, who am their Epitaph'. But these similarities only underline the differences, the difference in tone above all. In the case of the 'Nocturnall' we need not suppose Donne's personal involvement. But we do need to notice that he has set up no opposition between the temper of the lover's feelings and that of the poetry. And where the lover of 'Twicknam Garden' tries to contract the world to his own state and, when he fails, sees everything as mocking him, the lover of the 'Nocturnall', though quite as unfortunate, can distinguish between his own condition ('nor will my Sunne renew') and that of other lovers, and can bid them 'Enjoy your summer all'. Again, where the one fancies himself in a dire state, the other is really *in* one. Yet he shows no desire to weep himself out of his humanity into plants and stones. Instead, he convinces us that 'by her death' (a graver matter, truly, than mere rejection) he has been deprived, and against his will, even of the life that plants and stones possess. And because everything in the poem persuades us to see this deprivation as a real and terrible one, he is invested with a dignity we miss, and are meant to miss, in the conventional lover of 'Twicknam Garden'.

But when everything needful has been said about Donne's attack on the conventions we still have to stress how much he did with their aid, and quite consciously. We see this especially, I think, in his use of hyperbole: again and again a particular example of hyperbole turns out on examination to be a conventional one re-worked; and this often means not subverted but carried even further. 'The Sunne Rising' is squarely founded on a conventional base, this time Ovidian rather than Petrarchan; and in 'The Canonization', while some of the conventional hyperbole is rejected (the extravagant sighs and tears, fevers and chills, noticed before), the central conceit is stock-in-trade: Love's Martyrs and the Religion of Love. Donne 'makes it new' by the treatment he gives to it.

I want to look more closely at this poem, one of Donne's greatest triumphs. Here the poetry again makes us aware of conventional extravagance, but only in passing; this is a poem of the positive kind I have already spoken of, and in examining it we shall be seeing not only a remarkable single poem, but one which represents much of what Donne (and with him Shakespeare) did to give English love poetry a new significance and reality. There are several aspects to this success, and indeed it is the varied range of the poetry here which must be emphasized, the number of different but related things it is doing simultaneously, effects we find scattered if at all in the work of the sonneteers.[1]

One of the chief things to notice is how thoroughly dramatic the poem is, and with what dexterity the first words set up its dramatic situation. The speaker's outburst, 'For Godsake hold your tongue, and let me love,' is clearly a reply to someone who has been remonstrating with him about his love affair. But the reply, though impatient and explosive, is tempered with humour, and the humour, partly at the speaker's own expense ('Or chide my palsie,

---

[1] In this discussion of 'The Canonization' I am indebted at several points to Cleanth Brooks' analysis: see 'The Language of Paradox' in *The Well Wrought Urn* (London, 1968), pp. 7–16.

or my gout,/My five gray haires, or ruin'd fortune flout'),
is one aspect of a larger agility of mind: we find it in his
lively sense of the world around him, a world he can consider well lost for love. It is part of the strategy of the poem
that the speaker should display such a reassuring knowledge
of the world: here is a man who has looked about him, a
'judicious sharp spectator', and made his choice in full
awareness of the other passions of mankind. Because we see
this we can give more weight to what he says of that choice.

The language of this first stanza calls for comment too.
Not only does its vigour of diction and, more especially, of
movement create much of the trust we place in the persona's
judgment: beyond that, we notice the agile and fluid suggestiveness of the language.

> Or the Kings reall, or his stamped face
> Contemplate, what you will, approve.

The word 'reall' represents in microcosm the rapidly metamorphic nature of the language throughout the poem. From
one point of view the line is saying: Contemplate (a sly
word that, in any case) the King's actual, royal face or its
likeness on a coin; in other words: Go to Court or make a
fortune, or perhaps both; or even (in 'stamped face/Con-
template'): Turn into a miser. But 'reall', as well as meaning 'actual', is the name of a coin (see also Donne's play on
the word 'angel' in 'The Bracelet'), so that the monetary
sense of the word is already present before the line moves
from the court to the counting-house.

As we enter the second stanza the tone is noticeably
modulating; and indeed no poem of Donne's equals this in
its progression of tone: a development from impatience to
engrossment in joyful praise. The speaker gradually forgets
his irritation as he warms to his subject; by the time we
reach stanza three (the exact centre of the poem) the

modulation is complete. In stanza two we find a tone some-
where between that of the second half of the poem and that
of the opening. The explosiveness of 'For Godsake hold
your tongue...' has softened to 'Alas, alas, who's injur'd
by my love?' but the relation between the two is clear. The
humorous mockery of the second stanza is aimed both at the
critic's disapproval and at the stage-properties of conventional poetic love: Spenser's tradeful merchants lose no
ships through the lover's storm of sighs, no farmer's crops
or soil are ruined by his tears (and as one of my students
remarked, tears, being salt, would be especially ruinous to
cultivation). The conceited variations on the old metaphor
continue: the Petrarchan chills and fevers delay no spring,
add no new names to the bills of mortality. The getting-
and-spending world of stanza one returns in the next lines,
and with the poem's characteristic ambiguity:

> Soldiers finde warres, and Lawyers finde out still
> Litigious men, which quarrels move,
> Though she and I do love.

They get what they want, and look at it! (Compare them
with us, whose happiness they ignore.) Soldiers find wars,
but the sentence can also be read in reverse: wars find
soldiers, they find each other, being made for each other.
Lawyers still (or always) find litigious men, or find still-
litigious men, and the ambiguous 'which' ('who' or
'whom') allows two things to be said of them: they are
men *who move quarrels* as well as men *whom quarrels move*. The
language weds them indissolubly to their activity.

The opening of the third stanza, 'Call us what you will',
gives us the last glimpse, as it were, of the critic. The lover
will accommodate even a criticism to the celebration of his
love, which is now thoroughly under way. And here the
richness, the unified diversity, the metamorphic agility of

the language 'gathers to a greatness'. The whole stanza identifies the lovers with a succession of things that burn or fly,[1] the energetic and unforced dexterity of the wit twisting the two strands of imagery into an intricate knot at the centre of the stanza, which is also the centre of the poem. Call us flies, circling around each other's flame: I'll grant that (the lover says), and its implication too: each of us being a flame is burning himself out. On either view, both must perish. But the lover says: 'at our owne *cost*', not 'costs', for what can be said of one lover can be said of the other, and when the next line moves from flies to emblematic birds, 'And wee in us finde the'Eagle and the Dove', we are not only ascending from insects to birds: the verbal structure forbids us to identify either lover solely with either bird. The words 'in us' intimate that each is the Eagle and the Dove, that the two are one, and the one, two. Here we find, of course, yet another aspect of the 'language of paradox' which the poem so eloquently speaks. And as if to drive this meaning home, the next lines spell it out even while they move us a plane higher, from ordinary symbolic birds to the mythical, unique bird in which contraries are resolved, male and female, death and resurrection. The ascension of the images is also a fusion of the two kinds of image, since the Phoenix is both winged and aflame. And if it is one, that is, not two creatures but a single creature, and the one creature of its kind, the lovers too are one, 'are it'. This is the 'crowned knot of fire' to which the stanza has been building, and its extravagance is characteristic and intended seriously.

> The Phoenix ridle hath more wit
> By us, we two being one, are it.

The poem makes (almost degrades) the Phoenix riddle into

[1] And flies (see Lear's remark) do both.

a prophetic 'type' of the two lovers: they are not illustra-
tions of *it*, *it* is an inadequate representation of *them*.
'Princes do but play *us*': it is the same kind of startling
reversal, and yet, we are persuaded, it simply puts things
the right way round. And because the two are one, and 'so'
are what the phoenix *symbolizes*, both sexes blend in 'one
neutral thing'; not neuter, but at once Eagle and Dove.
Sex, of course, is not annihilated: 'the hee and shee' are not
forgotten, but become a third being, a neutral thing, free
presumably of the limitations of either sex. In this new
state of being,

> We dye and rise the same, and prove
> Mysterious by this love.

The word 'mysterious' tells us that the lovers have entered
the dimension of sanctity promised by the title. And the
parallel sets of meanings are especially striking: we die and
rise as saints and martyrs do (or, more immediately, as their
emblem and ours, the phoenix); and afterwards we are
what we were. But also: we go to bed together, make love
together, and we are what we were, undiminished by the
act of love. (The doubleness of the passage, of course,
depends on the sexual meaning of 'die'; Cleanth Brooks
surely protested more than he need have done on this
point.) But 'the same', of course, means not only 'un-
altered' but 'identical'. If *one* dies and rises, in whatever
sense, so too must the other; they are two and one: two
in the one flesh and the one mystery.

For my present purpose, which is to discuss not only the
nature of Donne's love poetry but the kind of love, the
awareness of love it embodies, we need go no further in this
poem. It is the middle stanza which defines and affirms so
triumphantly Donne's sense of the selfhood of lovers and

the fusion of two selfhoods in the relationship of love. Both words need to be used: 'selfhood' and 'relationship'. It is not to the point to say that we know nothing of the woman's personality, for we never for a moment doubt her existence or the reality of the state the poem expresses. The particulars are plainly unimportant: what matters is that there are two selves, and that in love they enter into a relationship by which the two are one; union without annihilation, and, as the last stanza suggests ('who did the whole worlds soule contract'), 'concentration without elimination'. Helen Gardner is quite right in saying that 'To have imagined and given supreme expression to the bliss of fulfilment, and to the discovery of the safety that there is in love given and returned, is Donne's greatest glory as a love-poet.'[1] Not that the 'bliss of fulfilment' is of the essence of Donne's achievement. That is only one manifestation of something more general: the sense of a profound, keen and urgent self-awareness, of a self confronting not only its own many-sidedness but the fact of other selves.

Some people, it is true, take exception to Donne's 'masculine perswasive force', to the arrogance of 'the Donne personality': surely, they feel, this is insulting to the mistress. Yet even when she is subjected to male arrogance, she clearly exists, she really is there; and this is a sense that few love poets give us, even good ones. The absence of the mistress suggests, often, a serious limitation in the imaginative range. Compare, for instance, Daniel's 'Faire is my Love' (discussed in the previous chapter) with Donne's 'Lecture upon the Shadow':

> Stand still, and I will read to thee
> A Lecture, Love, in loves philosophy.

[1] *The Elegies and the Songs and Sonnets*, Introduction, p. xxx.

Despite Donne's peremptory tone, a more genuine compliment is being paid than by Daniel's insipid lyricism.
Donne's mistress may reply that she'll be damned if she'll
stand still, but there can be no doubt in our minds that she
is there, nor in hers that she is really being addressed. And
the command leaves her free to retort with whatever spirit
she has in her. The realism of Donne's method makes us
feel that here again there are two actual people and a
relationship between them. Dryden's famous comment on
Donne is quite wrong, I think, especially in what it supposes
about women. Those mistresses *may* have been perplexed in
their fair minds, but they should certainly have been flattered (if also at times infuriated) by being so addressed.
The nice speculations in philosophy don't really leave them
out, and Donne has to be unusually disenchanted before he
will say, 'Hope not for minde in women': as a rule he proceeds as if it were there. Whereas Daniel's mistress, if she
could be supposed to exist, could only say (and rightly):
You're only interested in yourself and your poetry. And in
the exchange between C.S Lewis and Joan Bennett, it is
Mrs Bennett, I think, who has the best of it here:

It may be that 'any sensible woman' would rather be told of 'Thy
bared snow and thy unbraided gold,' but I am not sure. She can see
that in her looking-glass, or she may believe she sees these things
reflected in the work of some painter, for the painter's art can show
such things better than any words. It may interest her more to
know what it feels like to be a man in love.[1]

What this feels like is the main concern of Donne's
poetry, even more than it is of Shakespeare's. And at this
point I have to qualify what I said earlier through some

[1] Joan Bennett, 'The Love Poetry of John Donne, a Reply to Mr C.S.
Lewis' in William R. Keast (ed.), *Seventeenth Century English Poetry,
Modern Essays in Criticism* (New York, 1962), pp. 112–13.

words of C.S. Lewis's. While it is true that 'In certain senses of the word "love", Shakespeare is not so much our best as our only love poet',[1] from another point of view it will seem that of all the poets of his time, Donne is the only true *love* poet, the only one concerned with dramatizing the *experience* of love. By comparison with the other sonneteers, Shakespeare in the Sonnets is strikingly dramatic; by comparison with Donne he is much less so, and his poetry is at a noticeable remove from the situations and emotions on which it is working.

But this is a relative judgment only. What distinguishes them both and makes them allies is their realism, in either sense of the word. Perhaps it is easier to see this in the case of Donne, whose artistic realism – a matter of 'technique' – is dictated by a view of the world, of love, and of poetry about love, which is realistic in the more popular sense. Not that this means a more pedestrian view of love than that of the 'whining' poets whom he mocks, who 'have no Mistresse but their Muse'. On the contrary, we must notice, with Alvarez (and equally with Cruttwell), 'the skill by which he created a poetic language in which technique was at the service of a fullness of the intelligence', so that 'the final impression is one of a peculiarly heightened dignity'.[2] Nor would I exclude the more savage poems (such as 'Loves Alchymie') from this description.

With the reservation that the Sonnets are less fully dramatic, the same things can be said of Shakespeare. He too asserts the standard of common sense, of human reality, of the human person in love, and we may speak of dignity here, too, with at least an equal conviction.

Yet despite all they share, despite all those qualities

[1] *English Literature in the Sixteenth Century*, p. 505.
[2] A. Alvarez, *The School of Donne* (London, 1961), pp. 14–15.

which make them the pre-eminent love poets of their age, there are important ways in which they stand in contrast to each other, and are complementary rather than alike. One is struck by differences between the two poetic temperaments, and some discussion of these should help us to see more clearly what Shakespeare's poetic temperament was like, and to consider the relation between the love and the poetry of the Sonnets, between Shakespeare's experience and his art.

There is, of course, some danger of confusing the poetic self and the biographical self, that of the poems and that of the poet, and this is perhaps greater with Shakespeare than with Donne, since in the Sonnets Shakespeare speaks in the character of a lover who is also a poet. We cannot know how closely the poet in the Sonnets corresponds with the poet who wrote them, and it would be easy to fall into just another, if more subtle, form of the heresy that insists on relating the Sonnets to events in Shakespeare's life. I would agree, nevertheless, that while the Sonnets tell us little or nothing of an autobiographical nature, they do reveal something essential to the artistic personality from which the whole of his work proceeds, and without which it could not have been what it is.

When we put Donne and Shakespeare side by side, Donne's poetic self appears the more assertive, the more obviously 'dramatic', certainly the more self-dramatizing, aggressive even when most disheartened; Shakespeare's the more modest, the more self-effacing, one might say the more humble, though this (as I have argued earlier) does not imply total self-depreciation. About Donne it has often been said that though his poems are compressed dramas he would probably not have made a good playwright: 'It is not likely', as John Crowe Ransom remarks, 'that John

Donne could have written Shakespeare's plays'.[1] In any case, great frequenter of plays that he was, he seems to have written none of his own, and perhaps wisely. For, however diverse the moods and attitudes of the poems, the central figure is nearly always Donne himself – notwithstanding the 'dramatic monologues', for even in these, and they do show a Donne who is more than usually ready to assume a role 'out there', the flavour of his personality remains very strong. He is, as it were, pulling on a large, black, melancholy hat, with face to match, and yet remaining himself. A quick reminder of how totally Shakespeare transforms himself successively into his characters – those, say, of Lear, Othello and Leontes – will make the limits of Donne's dramatizations clearer. Indeed it is one of the most profound instincts of his nature to resist giving up the self, merging it with other selves, however aware he may be of others. Here a remark of Empson's is relevant: 'In the *Holy Sonnet* "I am a little world made cunningly"...I think the remorseful hope of atonement with God is crossed with a shrinking hunger for annihilation and escape from God.'[2] This is what has happened, in the Divine Poems, to the earlier self-assertion. It is such a diverse and interesting self: how could he wish to give it up, or even to go out of it for more than five minutes at a time?

Shakespeare, by contrast, is by no means so self-insistent, and here 'Shakespeare' means not only the poet-figure in the Sonnets but also the author of the work.

> Noe Longer mourne for me when I am dead ...
> Nay if you read this line, remember not,
> The hand that writ it.

[1] John Crowe Ransom, 'Shakespeare at Sonnets' in *The World's Body* (Baton Rouge, 1968), p. 271.
[2] William Empson, 'Donne and the Rhetorical Tradition', in Paul S. Alpers (ed.), *Elizabethan Poetry* (New York, 1967), p. 71.

The Sonnets do what the lover here recommends the friend to do. The wish on the lover's part is one index of Shakespeare's *artistic* ability to forget himself. About Sonnet 73, too, there is something characteristic both of the sequence and of Shakespeare's work as a whole:

> That time of yeeare thou maist in me behold,
> When yellow leaves, or none, or few doe hange
> Upon those boughes which shake against the could,
> Bare ruin'd quiers, where late the sweet birds sang.

We never forget that the images in each of this sonnet's quatrains are defining the speaker's state, and his sense of it, but we are more aware, as he is, of the things he takes to express it. In the lines quoted, it is surprising how quickly the 'I' ceases to be the centre of attention, for the speaker as well as for us: the poet dissolves into the images of his state and they in turn into images which illuminate *them*. They are so profoundly expressive of the poet's condition that he can lose himself in them. And in this, I think, we see the nature of Shakespeare's creativity, the nature of the genius which produced the plays: in the willingness to let other beings speak for him, and still more for themselves. At the risk of hackneyed repetition I must quote two passages from Keats' letters in which he clearly has Shakespeare as much as himself in mind:

It struck me, what quality went to form a Man of Achievement especially in Literature & which Shakespeare posessed so enormously – I mean *Negative Capability*, that is when man is capable of being in uncertainties, Mysteries, doubts, without any irritable reaching after fact & reason...[1]

As to the poetical Character...it is not itself – it has no self – it is every thing and nothing – It has no character – it enjoys light and

---

[1] Letter to George and Tom Keats, 27(?) December 1817, in *Letters of John Keats*, ed. H.E. Rollins (Cambridge, Mass., 1958), vol. I, p. 193.

shade; it lives in gusto, be it foul or fair, high or low, rich or poor, mean or elevated – It has as much delight in conceiving an Iago as an Imogen... A Poet is the most unpoetical of any thing in existence; because he has no Identity – he is continually... filling some other Body – The Sun, the Moon, the Sea and Men and Women who are creatures of impulse are poetical and have about them an unchangeable attribute – the poet has none; no identity – he is certainly the most unpoetical of all God's Creatures.[1]

It need hardly be said how much more accurately these passages describe Shakespeare than Donne, or how well they single out a quality which Shakespeare possessed to an extraordinary degree: the gift of empathy. He was 'continually filling some other body'. What the lover of the Sonnets is in his love, Shakespeare is in his work. In the plays he is 'everywhere present and everywhere hidden', showing in the fullest measure what Stephen Dedalus means by the dramatic artist. So that it may at first seem strange that the Sonnets themselves are not more fully dramatic. They are, in fact, remarkably *un*-dramatic, if we compare them with the plays or with Donne. Even if the poet in the Sonnets is a creation rather than Shakespeare himself, he is less fully created than the characters of the plays. Is this simply because Shakespeare in writing lyrics hears no call for fuller characterization, or is it rather that for him a mask is indispensable and that the speaker in these poems does not provide an adequate mask, is not sufficiently distanced? For it is something more than a naive tendency to identify the 'I' of the poems with Shakespeare himself that makes us persist in feeling an affinity between them. In the Sonnets Shakespeare does not unlock his heart or that of the lover–poet as he unlocks that of Lear or Macbeth. It is natural for him, I think, to work not through im-

[1] Letter to Richard Woodhouse, 27 October 1818, in *Letters*, vol. I, pp. 386–7.

mediate relationships but through apparently more remote ones: fully externalized figures whom he can enter and animate and become.

Yet it will be clear how closely the lover's gifts, as he reveals them in the poems, resemble those of Shakespeare's creative genius itself. C.S. Lewis, in a passage already quoted, speaks of 'this patience... this transference of the whole self into another self without the demand for a return', and the word 'patience' sends us back to Keats. If it is the plays which show how fully Shakespeare possessed 'negative capability' and the 'poetical character', the Sonnets, too, bear witness to it in their own way. And part of that way is the kind of love they utter. If, as many readers think, the Sonnets are among the most *mature* love poems in the language, it is largely because of this patience: the willingness to feel one's way through a situation rather than to impose oneself masterfully upon it. The address, the posture, are the antithesis to Donne's, and whatever of Donne's vividness and immediacy may be lacking, there are rewards which Donne's poetry cannot offer. 'Wise' is not a word one hastens to apply to Donne's love poetry (though neither, of course, is 'foolish'); but Shakespeare's Sonnets do suggest that patience in love is the beginning of wisdom.

6

Art as a Mode of Love

'Leaving thee living in posterity'
(Sonnet 6)

Patience, however, is not inertia, and 'negative capability' denotes no more than the conditions from which poetic activity may start. Love by its very nature is productive: in the Sonnets, the youth must beget a child and the poet who loves him must find the proper expression for his love. The poem, of course, is his offspring; his mode of love is art. Here some well-known phrases apply: his interest in his experience will be inseparable from his interest in words, poetry will come as naturally as leaves to a tree. The speaker in the sonnets to the youth is as much a figure of the poet as of the lover; the two roles are aspects of the one nature. The poet aspect becomes clear even in the first set of sonnets, though these are less interested in poems than in children; and the concern voiced there, with the engrafting of beauty into language, only grows as the sequence proceeds. And if it is natural in a poet for love to lead to art, it is inevitable in an Elizabethan poet contemplating love against the 'mutability' with which his age was so urgently concerned. The poet's task is to halt the flux of time as far as he can, to commemorate the fleeting life of the beloved in monuments more lasting than bronze. Shakespeare attempts it again and again, with varying results but at his best with far greater success than any of his contemporaries: a success

144

due to the fact that he brings to the task more modesty and good sense, a finer intelligence.

But to show how this idea is introduced into the sequence, I must return to what I said in chapter 1 about the later sonnets in the first group. Where Sonnet 12 merely warns the youth that 'nothing gainst Times sieth can make defence/Save breed to brave him, when he takes thee hence', Sonnet 15 finds something further to say; and it comes at the end of a poem squarely confronting the facts of mutability.

> And all in war with Time for love of you
> As he takes from you, I ingraft you new.

The next sonnet, working dialectically against this, returns to the idea of begetting children:

> But wherefore do not you a mightier waie
> Make warre uppon this bloudie tirant time?

'A mightier waie'? From one point of view it is; and it is from this point of view that the poet now speaks of his 'barren rime'. Shakespeare puts life above art, as Wilson Knight has said; and pursuing this bias towards life and the living, 'the breathers of this world', he is concerned in the next sonnet with the voice of posterity: that, too, matters, since it has to do with the living.

> Who will beleeve my verse in time to come?

It may well

> Be scorn'd, like old men of lesse truth then tongue,
> And your true rights be termd a Poets rage,
> And stretched miter of an Antique song.

So what this sonnet proposes is a concerted effort, from poet and youth alike:

> But were some childe of yours alive that time,
> You should live twise, in it and in my rime.[1]

After this we hear no more of propagation: the focus shifts. Shakespeare is of course not just contradicting himself. He is exploring the virtues, that is the powers, of each immortality; and also the defects of each. People do matter more than poems; nevertheless, in the long perspectives of history, in which devouring time will blunt the lion's paws and whole families may die out completely, great poetry, if the page on which it is written survives, 'may still shine bright' (Sonnet 65).

With Sonnet 18 ('Shall I compare thee to a Summers day?') we come to the first of the full-scale immortalizations. Its strategy should be kept in mind in the discussion which follows, for it makes us aware, by the comparison it poses and then appears to reject, of the quality of the youth's beauty, its golden and transient perfection, held like a mote in a late sunbeam. So he appears in the order of nature; but there is the other order, for the sestet to affirm. 'Art is Art', as Yeats reminds us, 'because it is not Nature'.

> But thy eternall Sommer shall not fade,
> Nor loose possession of that faire thou ow'st,
> Nor shall death brag thou wandr'st in his shade,
> When in eternall lines to time thou grow'st,
> So long as men can breath or eyes can see,
> So long lives this, and this gives life to thee.

'I will make you immortal', or sometimes, 'I have made you immortal': the claim, so often made, so often strikes us now as a hollow boast which one poem after another fails to make good. In what sense can a poem immortalize the beloved? Consider for a moment a twentieth-century des-

---

[1] I have amended the punctuation of the Quarto in this line.

cendant of the Elizabethan poems on this subject: Yeats'
early-middle poem 'A Woman Homer Sung'.

> Whereon I wrote and wrought,
> And now, being grey,
> I dream that I have brought
> To such a pitch my thought
> That coming time can say,
> 'He shadowed in a glass
> What thing her body was.'

But did he? The poem tells us only that

> she had fiery blood
> When I was young,
> And trod so sweetly proud
> As 'twere upon a cloud,
> A woman Homer sung,
> That life and letters seem
> But an heroic dream.[1]

How ambiguously does Yeats intend that favourite word
'shadowed'? Does it hint that the best that poetry can do
is to show the beloved body 'in a glass darkly'? How fully
can art re-embody that incarnate beauty? There is a characteristic, and realistic, trace of doubt in the poet's mind: 'I
dream that I have brought/To such a pitch my thought'.
The poem's affirmation is a qualified one.

Reading the Elizabethans on this theme, one could wish
that that were far more often the case. There is much vapid
confidence and a good deal of bombast. As Archibald Mac-
Leish found:

> The praisers of women in their proud and beautiful poems,
> Naming the grave mouth and the hair and the eyes,
> Boasted those they loved should be forever remembered:
> These were lies.

[1] W. B. Yeats, *Collected Poems* (London, 1950), p. 100.

The words sound but the face in the Istrian sun is forgotten.[1]

When Daniel tells Delia:

> But I must sing of thee and those faire eies,
> Autentique shall my verse in time to come,
> When yet th'vnborne shall say, Lo where she lies,
> Whose beauty made him speake that els was dombe.
>
> (*Delia*, XLVI)

the verse with its smooth emptiness leaves us unpersuaded: how can those fair eyes authenticate his verse, in time to come *or* now? This sort of thing is fairly typical, and not only of Daniel. On the other hand, in a couple of lines by Drayton:

> And Queenes hereafter shall be glad to live
> Upon the Almes of thy superfluous prayse,
>
> (*Idea*, 6)

the swell and sweep of the verse are strangely convincing. We are told nothing about the woman, given no evidence that she is worth remembering except the movement and ring of the poetry. This does convey something of the lover's passion, if nothing of the woman's uniqueness, and the tone persuades us to take that on trust.

One must accept the fact that these poets do not consider making a *portrait* of the beloved: they don't fail to do this, they never attempt it. 'Shall I compare thee to a Summers day?' comes as close to it as any sonnet of its time; for obviously such poems as Spenser's 'Ye tradefull Merchants' (to name only one of the better examples) are

---

[1] Archibald MacLeish, 'Not Marble nor the Guilded Monuments' (1930), in his *Collected Poems* (Boston, 1962), p. 58. At the end of his own poem he makes an attempt to put things right:
I will not speak of the famous beauty of dead women:
I will say the shape of a leaf lay once on your hair.
Till the world ends and the eyes are out and the mouths broken
Look! It is there!

not concerned with drawing the mistress's likeness or suggesting in precise terms her personal qualities. The question
must be asked: What did these poets, including Shakespeare, mean when they claimed that their verse would
confer immortality; what did they expect the poem itself to
achieve?

It is sometimes said that their true subject is not the
mistress at all but the power of art. This is too simple a
view. Why, after all, is a mistress mentioned at all? Even
though the poems are concerned chiefly with poetry, the
mistress is, or should be, an essential element. The best
poems show this; in others the inferiority of the poetry can
partly be traced to the fact that the poet has not convinced
us of her existence, or of her importance to him. Even in
Daniel's superficial treatment of the convention (already
quoted) we can see its central and minimal meaning: the
mistress, simply by *being*, and by being precious in the
poet's eyes, is the breath of his inspiration. Her life is
'grafted new' on the tree of his art; but more than this, the
tree owes to her the life it has, and that life is an enduring
one. So at the root of the convention is a recognition of the
poet's debt to that particular 'muse', his mistress, as well
as of the power of the art which results from her influence.
Or which may result: for sometimes we feel that the poem
is referring not so much to itself as to other poems, perhaps
not yet written, 'where I to thee Eternitie shall give'
(Drayton, *Idea*, 6); where the possibility, so far merely
asserted, will be seen realized.

There are difficulties for a modern reader, perhaps for any
reader, in accepting many of these poems. It may be too
much to ask that the poet give us a portrait of the beloved,
but surely we should feel that for him she exists and matters
as a unique person: this, after all, is part of the poem's

'invention', and he shouldn't be let off with a paper doll instead of a bird in the hand. Further, the poem which promises immortality should strike us as actually carrying out its promise, and this will depend on two things: not only on its creation of that sense of the beloved which I have been stressing, but on the firmness with which it builds her verbal monument then and there.

To return to Shakespeare and to his handling of the theme. Often enough he too leaves us unconvinced, as in the couplet of Sonnet 60 ('Like as the waves make towards the pibled shore'):

> And yet to times in hope, my verse shall stand
> Praising thy worth, dispight [Time's] cruell hand.

This is far too perfunctory, and indeed, gives the whole idea no more than a brief nod. And when he addresses 'swift-footed time' in Sonnet 19:

> But I forbid thee one most hainous crime,
> O carve not with thy howers my loves faire brow,

one may well ask, out of its context, Wilson Knight's question: 'Is there any point at all in talking like this?'[1] For the command is plainly absurd, as the speaker himself must recognize, and the conclusion to which he retreats seems, in its facile way, unsatisfactory also:

> Yet doe thy worst ould Time dispight thy wrong,
> My love shall in my verse ever live young.

Far profounder and more considerable are those sonnets in which the poet sets poetic immortality in a context of death and decay which have been genuinely confronted. And here the claims made for poetry sound very differently:

[1] *The Mutual Flame*, p. 76.

in some cases tempered, in others strengthened, by the spectacle which the poetry presents of time's ravages. Sometimes the dominant thought is: Can art possibly defeat such an enemy as this? At others, and only rarely, the mood is one of earned confidence: the ravages of time and the power of art are held in the one thought and presented with equal imaginative force.

Two sonnets already discussed in chapter 3 should be mentioned again, though neither is in the full sense an 'immortalization'. Sonnet 124 ('Yf my deare love were but the childe of state') does something comparable to immortalizing the beloved: it immortalizes the poet's love for the friend, and the power of this love to stand outside the 'state' of time and of arbitrary change:

> No it was buylded far from accident,
> It suffers not in smilinge pomp, nor falls
> Under the blow of thralled discontent,
> Whereto th'inviting time our fashion calls:
> It feares not policy that *Heriticke*,
> Which workes on leases of short numbred howers,
> But all alone stands hugely pollitick,
> That it nor growes with heat, nor drownes with showres.

We find here the measured, authoritative exaltation of tone of those few sonnets which convincingly claim in the friend's behalf a triumph over mortality. Again, Sonnet 71 needs to be considered afresh in the present context:

> Noe Longer mourne for me when I am dead,
> Then you shall heare the surly sullen bell
> Give warning to the world that I am fled
> From this vile world with vildest wormes to dwell:
> Nay if you read this line, remember not,
> The hand that writ it, for I love you so,
> That I in your sweet thoughts would be forgot,
> If thinking on me then should make you woe.

O if (I say) you looke upon this verse,
When I (perhaps) compounded am with clay,
Do not so much as my poore name reherse;
But let your love even with my life decay.
  Least the wise world should looke into your mone,
  And mocke you with me after I am gon.

I have already discussed the quality of the poet's love as it is expressed here, its extraordinary generosity and self-forgetfulness. In this it goes to the furthest extreme, above all in lines 7 and 8. One should also notice that as in Drayton's lines ('And Queenes hereafter...') we learn nothing about the beloved, but the lover's tone and disposition give us all we need in order to accept the friend and his significance. His reflection in the lover is enough, because the poetry creates it. But more to the present purpose, though less noticeable, is the poet's consciousness of himself and of his poem. He is present both as the man whose end the 'surly sullen bell' will eventually toll and as the poet whose verse will remain when he, and perhaps the friend's love for him, are gone. Though we find extreme self-renunciation, there is no lack of self-awareness, or awareness of his writing:

Nay if you read this line, remember not,
The hand that writ it...

O if (I say) you looke upon this verse.

There is humility here, but no false humility. These gestures may carry an almost unbearable pathos, but they are not pathetic attempts at self-assurance. There is no nervous fingering of the 'verse' to see if it is still there and if it is going to be lasting enough; no suspicion that the poet is taking solace from it. There is, however, an assumption, effortlessly implied and as readily accepted, that 'this verse' itself will survive, and perhaps long after its advice is taken and the poet–lover has been forgotten.

Among the numerous sonnets which are, marginally or centrally, immortalizations, Sonnet 107 ('Not mine owne feares') should be added to those already mentioned, especially for the thought in its last six lines:

> Now with the drops of this most balmie time,
> My love lookes fresh, and death to me subscribes,
> Since spight of him Ile live in this poore rime,
> While he insults ore dull and speachlesse tribes.
> And thou in this shalt finde thy monument,
> When tyrants crests and tombs of brasse are spent.

Here is the calm opposition of 'death' and 'poore rime', the adjective suggesting, obliquely and powerfully, the contempt in which death is held in this moment of confident and visionary expansion. And here, too, are the twin assertions:

> Ile live in this poore rime,

and

> thou in this shalt finde thy monument;

the one self-regarding, with a hint of Ovid's vein ('my name will be imperishable. Wherever Roman power extends over the lands Rome has subdued, people will read my verse'),[1] the other looking, in the manner of Sonnet 18, to the friend. If I call attention to the 'thought' of the sonnet it is because this is a matter of valid interest in any study of the handling of this subject; it seems to me, however, that the poem does not give it enough poetic life to satisfy us completely.

There are three sonnets, above all, which show the extent of Shakespeare's achievement with this theme. Not all of

---

[1] Ovid, *Metamorphoses*, XV, closing lines. Translated by Mary M. Innes (Harmondsworth, 1955), p. 388.

them are by Shakespeare: two are his and the third is by Spenser. Taken together in a certain order they mark a progression towards the greatest inclusiveness which the immortalization poem was to attain. To begin with, Shakespeare's Sonnet 65:

> Since brasse, nor stone, nor earth, nor boundlesse sea,
> But sad mortallity ore-swaies their power,
> How with this rage shall beautie hold a plea,
> Whose action is no stronger then a flower?
> O how shall summers hunny breath hold out,
> Against the wrackfull siedge of battring dayes,
> When rocks impregnable are not so stoute,
> Nor gates of steele so strong but time decayes?
> O fearefull meditation, where alack,
> Shall times best Jewell from times chest lie hid?
> Or what strong hand can hold his swift foote back,
> Or who his spoile of beautie can forbid?
>   O none, unlesse this miracle have might,
>   That in black inck my love may still shine bright.

The tremendous strength of the first twelve lines is obvious; one may come more slowly to accept the final couplet. Indeed I once thought it one of the disappointing couplets discussed in chapter 4, but I no longer think so. For what the poem exists to say is that amid such universal ruin as it contemplates, beauty can have no chance of preservation unless a miracle occurs: most of the imaginative weight must fall, then, on the 'rage', the 'wrackfull siedge' of mortality, and on the defencelessness of beauty's 'flower' and 'summers hunny breath'; the poem's ending is therefore deliberately and properly tentative. There is nothing here of the facile optimism we have seen elsewhere. Instead, full recognition is given to the spectacle described; the exclamation, 'O fearefull meditation', dominates the rest of the poem's thought. Nothing is *asserted* in the couplet, except a possibility ('O none, unlesse...'), and even that, the poem admits, will require a miracle. Perhaps there is *something* more than this: the insinuation that the poem itself may be 'this miracle', may have the 'might' spoken of; but it is nothing like an explicit claim. A backward glance at Sonnet 60 will show this by contrast: 'And yet to times in hope, my verse shall stand'. The end of 65 is stronger precisely because it *is* so tentative. Further, it should be clear how much more *intelligent* this poem is than Sonnet 60 and some others: it accepts its own logic, without trying at the end to ignore the disturbing realities it has faced earlier.

But it does not follow that this powerfully sombre view is the only intelligent one a poet might take. Shakespeare is here looking at the whole question under its darkest aspect, but there are others. One of Spenser's best-known sonnets takes a more sanguine view:

> One day I wrote her name vpon the strand,
>> but came the waues and washed it away:
>> agayne I wrote it with a second hand,
>> but came the tyde, and made my paynes his pray.
> Vayne man, sayd she, that doest in vaine assay,
>> a mortall thing so to immortalize,
>> for I my selue shall lyke to this decay,
>> and eek my name bee wyped out lykewize.
> Not so, (quod I) let baser things deuize
>> to dy in dust, but you shall liue by fame:
>> my verse your vertues rare shall eternize,
>> and in the heuens wryte your glorious name.
> Where whenas death shall all the world subdew,
>> our loue shall liue, and later life renew.
>
> (*Amoretti*, LXXV)

In relation to the sonnet just discussed, this is clearly more hopeful, and yet it gives to its hopes less substance than the other gave to its fears. We can see quite plainly how much greater are the positive claims it makes for poetry, though their poetic force is not as great as it might be. The opening of the poem has a splendid vigour of movement, and the situation employed to the end of the octave gives the poem a firm dramatic outline: the lover scribbling away vainly (a sort of literary Canute?) in the path of the waves, and the woman there beside him, rallying him in a pleasantly feminine manner on the vanity of his efforts, thus giving him the chance to reply in the sestet. When he does so, unfortunately, the bombast starts ('Not so, (quod I) let baser things deuize/to dy in dust'), the poetry thins out and fails to make good its own soaring claims. On the other hand, while the couplet's assertion seems hollow as stated, it does extend the *idea* of poetic immortalization in an interesting direction: beyond the simple 'you shall live by fame' of many poets, to 'our love shall live, and later life renew'. *How*, we are not told, and this is a weakness in the conclusion, but in a skeletal, merely intellectual form the poem offers the broader notion that an immortalization poem may somehow quicken generations to come.

And this is the point at which Spenser's sonnet connects with the last Shakespeare sonnet I want to consider. This poem synthesizes the actual or potential virtues of the other two: it has all the power of Sonnet 65 in picturing the ruins of time, and it gives sense and validity to all that Spenser's couplet says, and more besides.

> Not marble, nor the guilded monuments
> Of Princes shall out-live this powrefull rime,
> But you shall shine more bright in these contents
> Then unswept stone, besmeer'd with sluttish time.
> When wastefull warre shall *Statues* over-turne,
> And broiles roote out the worke of masonry,

Nor *Mars* his sword, nor warres quick fire shall burne:
The living record of your memory.
Gainst death, and all oblivious enmity
Shall you pace forth, your praise shall stil finde roome,
Even in the eyes of all posterity
That weare this world out to the ending doome.
    So til the judgement that your selfe arise,
    You live in this, and dwell in lovers eies.

This seems to me one of the four or five greatest of the Sonnets, and probably the greatest immortalization poem in the language.[1] Its rarity among poems of this kind lies in the way it brings together, in an artistic unity, themes and materials usually found scattered elsewhere, or not found at all. In every way, much more is happening here: the poem is so comprehensive that it seems to do as much as most of the others put together. Where 65 is a 'fearefull meditation' upon such widespread ruin that 'times best jewel' is almost (if not utterly) lost from sight, 55 can hold in equal imaginative balance both the general ruin and the particular beloved, and can relate him to all others who love and are loved; and it does this in terms which recognize them, too, as unique.

It is in every sense a monumental poem. Not only is most of its imagery concerned with monuments or memorials of some kind and with what may happen to them (statues, works of masonry, and perhaps also written records, which can be burnt along with buildings), but more important, the poem is as firmly 'builded' as any reader could wish it, and as it needs to be, if it is to be what it claims to be, a 'powrefull rime'. It must be seen to be stronger, in poetic terms, than the other monuments it must 'out-live'. (And that word is chosen, rather than 'outlast', to intimate that

---

[1] J. W. Lever in *The Elizabethan Love Sonnet*, pp. 246–72, anticipates some of what I say of this sonnet and of others on the same theme.

this monument has a quality not found in the others: it out-*lives* them by being the lover's own voice still alive in the poem, 'the living record of your memory'.) This poem not only *talks* of being a monument: because of the firmness of its making, it *is* one.

Some of its material seems to have been quarried from a Horace ode and the end of Ovid's *Metamorphoses*: what matters, of course, is Shakespeare's use of it. Where the Roman poets are celebrating their own immortality, Shakespeare lays his stress elsewhere and characteristically transforms his sources completely. The Romans say: Because of my poem *I* will never die. Shakespeare says: Because of my poem *you* will never die. Of course, plenty of his contemporaries made that amendment too; but here again, in the couplet, Shakespeare rings an all-important change on the received idea. Most poets are content to say: You are immortal in my poem. Spenser goes a step further: You are immortal in my poem, from which our love will reach out to enhance later lives. Shakespeare goes further again: You are immortal in my poem, and in yourself, and you will live in the poem, in yourself and in the eyes of later lovers. What distinguishes Shakespeare is that he values the identity of the beloved; he recognizes that the beloved has his own personal immortality, in no way dependent on poetry. Despite the claims made, and made good, for 'this powrefull rime', the poet looks beyond it to the personal resurrection of the friend at the end of time (prepared for by the phrase 'to the ending doome'):

> So til the judgement that *your selfe* arise.

It is obvious that the vision, unlike Horace's and Ovid's, is eschatological. Their conception of the future is a more limited one, concerned with a world which 'Rome has subdued'. The Christian after-life has given Shakespeare's imagination more to embrace. It is the couplet which finally confirms the breadth and range of Shakespeare's vision, his sense of two autonomous immortalities, the artistic and the personal. Of these, it is the personal which is the ultimate one. There will be a judgment day when the self will arise. Meanwhile, there is the temporary immortality of art, which witnesses to the beloved before the whole of time, this side of the ending doom. The limits, and therefore the modesty, of this claim should be evident. It is a modesty which makes Shakespeare's vision far more inclusive than that of any other poet treating the subject. The last line forms the culmination:

> You live in this, and dwell in lovers eies.

Within the dimension of time, the poem is not the only repository of the memory, the reality, of the beloved. 'You live in this', that is, in the poem; but equally (or perhaps still more), '[You] dwell in lovers eies'. 'Live' and 'dwell': they are not identical, the second word extends the first. While 'live' emphasizes the fact and the continuance of life, 'dwell' suggests the inwardness of that life to the 'lovers eies', and carries the sense of permanence, of habitation.[1] And the open form of the line's statement leaves it to us to decide (as Spenser's last line does not) what part the poem plays in this in-dwelling: whether the beloved dwells in the eyes of future lovers *who read the verse*, or in the eyes of all lovers simply because they *are* lovers, no matter whether they read it or not. So that it is not only the *verse* which resurrects the beloved within time; it is Love itself, as it happens repeatedly to the living, through generation

---

[1] See the last line of Jonson's 'To Penshurst': 'their lords have built, but thy lord dwells.' (*Poems*, ed. G. B. Johnston, p. 79).

after generation. The poet's beloved becomes, then, the image of love: *he* is what all lovers see when they look into each other's eyes.

This is the ultimate triumph of Shakespeare's mode of love: to make 'for short time an endlesse moniment' (in Spenser's fine words), and yet to see, and to say, that beyond both time and the poem, the beloved 'shall pace forth' in his own right, and in other lives, and not by virtue of any poetry whatever.

Bibliography

EDITIONS OF THE SONNETS

Beeching, H.C. *The Sonnets of Shakespeare*. Boston, 1904.

Brooke, Tucker. *Shakespeare's Sonnets*. Edited with introduction and notes. Oxford, 1936.

Ingram, W.G. and Redpath, Theodore. *Shakespeare's Sonnets*. London, 1967.

Rollins, Hyder Edward. *A New Variorum Edition of Shakespeare: The Sonnets*. 2 vols. Philadelphia and London, 1944.

Rowse, A.L. *Shakespeare's Sonnets*. Edited with an introduction and notes. London, 1964.

Seymour-Smith, Martin. *Shakespeare's Sonnets*. Edited with an introduction and commentary. London, 1963.

Tucker, T.G. *The Sonnets of Shakespeare*. Edited from the Quarto of 1609 with introduction and commentary. Cambridge, 1924.

Wilson, John Dover. *The Sonnets*. Edited with an introduction. Cambridge, 1966.

WORKS BY SIXTEENTH AND SEVENTEENTH CENTURY AUTHORS (CHIEFLY POETS)

Daniel, Samuel. *Poems and A Defence of Rhyme*. Edited by Arthur Colby Sprague. Chicago and London, 1965.

Donne, John. *The Poems of John Donne*. Edited by H.J.C. Grierson. 2 vols. Oxford, 1912.

The Elegies and the Songs and Sonnets. Edited with an introduction and commentary by Helen Gardner. Oxford, 1965.

Drayton, Michael. *The Works of Michael Drayton*. Edited by J. William Hebel. Oxford, 1961.

Jonson, Ben. *Poems*. Edited by G.B. Johnston. London, 1954.

Works. Edited by C.H. Herford and Percy Simpson. 11 vols. Oxford, 1954.

Lee, Sidney (ed.). *Elizabethan Sonnets*. 2 vols. with an introduction. New York, 1964.

Puttenham, George. *The Arte of English Poesie*. Edited by Edward Arber. Westminster, 1895.

Ralegh, Sir Walter. *The Poems of Sir Walter Ralegh*. Edited by Agnes Latham. London, 1962.

Sidney, Sir Philip. *The Poems of Sir Philip Sidney*. Edited by William A. Ringler, Jr. Oxford, 1962.

Spenser, Edmund. *The Poetical Works of Edmund Spenser*. Edited by J.C. Smith and E. de Selincourt. Oxford, 1957.

Wilson, Thomas. *The Arte of Rhetorique*. A facsimile reproduction, edited with an introduction by Robert Hood Bowers. Gainesville, Florida, 1962.

Wyatt, Sir Thomas. *Poems*. Edited by Kenneth Muir. London, 1949.

WORKS BY OTHER POETS

Hopkins, Gerard Manley. *The Poems of Gerard Manley Hopkins*. Edited by W.H. Gardner. Oxford, 1956.

Keats, John. *The Letters of John Keats*. Edited by H.E. Rollins. 2 vols. Cambridge, Mass., 1958.

MacLeish, Archibald. *Collected Poems*. Boston, 1962.

Ovid. *Metamorphoses*. Translated by Mary M. Innes. Harmondsworth, 1955.

Petrarca, Francesco. *Canzoniere*. Edited by Michele Scherillo. Milan, 1908.

Yeats, W.B. *Collected Poems*. London, 1950.

WORKS OF CRITICISM AND SCHOLARSHIP

Alpers, Paul J. (ed.). *Elizabethan Poetry: Modern Essays in Criticism*. New York, 1967.

Alvarez, A. *The School of Donne*. London, 1961.

Auden, W.H. Introduction to *The Sonnets* (Signet edition). New York, 1964.

Barber, C.L. 'An Essay on the Sonnets' in *The Sonnets* (Laurel Shakespeare). New York, 1962.

Bennett, Joan. 'The Love Poetry of John Donne, a Reply to Mr C.S. Lewis' in William R. Keast (ed.) *Seventeenth Century English Poetry, Modern Essays in Criticism*. New York, 1962.

Booth, Stephen. *An Essay on Shakespeare's Sonnets*. New Haven and London, 1969.

Brooks, Cleanth. *The Well Wrought Urn*. London, 1968.

Cruttwell, Patrick. *The Shakespearean Moment: and its Place in the Poetry of the Seventeenth Century*. New York, 1960.

Empson, William. 'Donne and the Rhetorical Tradition' in Paul S. Alpers (ed.) *Elizabethan Poetry: Modern Essays in Criticism*. New York, 1967.

   Seven Types of Ambiguity. Harmondsworth, 1961.

   Some Versions of Pastoral. Harmondsworth, 1966.

   The Structure of Complex Words. London, 1964.

Evans, Maurice. *English Poetry in the Sixteenth Century*. London, 1955.

Fiedler, Leslie A. 'Some Contexts of Shakespeare's Sonnets' in Edward Hubler (ed.) *The Riddle of Shakespeare's Sonnets*. New York, 1962.

Gardner, Helen (ed.). *The Elegies and the Songs and Sonnets of John Donne*. Edited with an introduction and commentary. Oxford, 1965.

Graves, Robert, and Riding, Laura. 'A Study in Original Spelling and Punctuation' (Sonnet 129) in Barbara Herrnstein (ed.) *Discussions of Shakespeare's Sonnets*. Boston, 1964.

Grundy, Joan. 'Shakespeare's Sonnets and the Elizabethan Sonneteers' in *Shakespeare Survey 15*, 1962.

Guss, Donald L. *John Donne, Petrarchist*. Detroit, 1966.

Herrnstein, Barbara (ed.). *Discussions of Shakespeare's Sonnets*. Edited and with an introduction. Boston, 1964.

Hotson, Leslie. *Mr. W.H.* London, 1954.

   Shakespeare's Sonnets Dated, and Other Essays. London, 1949.

Hubler, Edward (ed.). *The Riddle of Shakespeare's Sonnets*. New York, 1962.

Hubler, Edward. *The Sense of Shakespeare's Sonnets*. New York, 1952.

Johnson, Samuel. *Lives of the English Poets*. 2 vols. London, 1925.

Ker, W.P. *Form and Style in Poetry*. London, 1928.

Knight, G. Wilson. *The Crown of Life*. London, 1965.

   The Mutual Flame. London, 1955.

Knights, L.C. 'Shakespeare's Sonnets' in his *Explorations*. Harmondsworth, 1964.

   Some Shakespearean Themes. London, 1959.

Krieger, Murray. *A Window to Criticism: Shakespeare's Sonnets and Modern Poetics.* Princeton, 1964.

Landry, Hilton. *Interpretations in Shakespeare's Sonnets.* Berkeley and Los Angeles, 1963.

Leishman, J.B. *Themes and Variations in Shakespeare's Sonnets.* London, 1961.

Lever, J.W. *The Elizabethan Love Sonnet.* London, 1966.

Lewis, C.S. *English Literature in the Sixteenth Century (Excluding Drama).* Oxford, 1954.

Mahood, M.M. 'Love's Confin'd Doom' in *Shakespeare Survey* 15, 1962.

Shakespeare's Wordplay. London, 1957.

Mizener, Arthur. 'The Structure of Figurative Language in Shakespeare's Sonnets' in Barbara Herrnstein (ed.) *Discussions of Shakespeare's Sonnets.* Boston, 1964.

Nowottny, Winifred. 'Formal Elements in Shakespeare's Sonnets: Sonnets I–VI' in Barbara Herrnstein (ed.) *Discussions of Shakespeare's Sonnets.* Boston, 1964.

The Language Poets Use. London, 1962.

Peterson, Douglas L. *The English Lyric from Wyatt to Donne: A History of the Plain and Eloquent Styles.* Princeton, N.J., 1967.

'A Probable Source for Shakespeare's Sonnet CXXIX' in *Shakespeare Quarterly,* v, 4, 1954.

Prince, F.T. *Shakespeare: The Poems.* Writers and their Work Series. London, 1963.

Ransom, John Crowe. *The World's Body.* New edition, with Preface and Postscript. Baton Rouge, 1968.

Robertson, J.M. *The Problems of the Shakespeare Sonnets.* London, 1926.

Saintsbury, George. *History of English Prosody.* 3 vols. New York, 1961.

Schaar, Claes. *An Elizabethan Sonnet Problem.* Lund, 1960.

Elizabethan Sonnet Themes and the Dating of Shakespeare's 'Sonnets'. Lund, 1962.

Smith, A.J. *John Donne: The Songs and Sonets.* London, 1964.

Smith, Hallett. *Elizabethan Poetry: A Study in Conventions, Meaning and Expression.* Cambridge, Mass., 1952.

Tuve, Rosemond. *Elizabethan and Metaphysical Imagery.* Chicago, 1961.

Vickers, Brian. *Classical Rhetoric in English Poetry.* London, 1970.

BIBLIOGRAPHY

Willen, Gerald, and Reed, Victor B. *A Casebook on Shakespeare's Sonnets*. New York, 1964.

Wilson, J. Dover (ed.). *Hamlet*. Cambridge, 1936.

Winny, James. *The Master-Mistress: A Study of Shakespeare's Sonnets*. London, 1968.

Winters, Yvor. 'Poetic Style in Shakespeare's Sonnets' in Barbara Herrnstein (ed.) *Discussions of Shakespeare's Sonnets*. Boston, 1964.

OTHER WORKS REFERRED TO

Fromm, Erich. *The Art of Loving*. London, 1966.

Machiavelli, Niccolo. *The Discourses*. New York, 1950.

Rougemont, Denis de. *Passion and Society*. London, 1960.

Shaw, George Bernard. *The Dark Lady of the Sonnets*. Preface in *Prefaces by Bernard Shaw*. London, 1938.

Shakespeare's sonnets discussed

Index